SEARCHING FOR A PAST

THE ADOPTED ADULT'S UNIQUE
PROCESS OF FINDING IDENTITY

JAYNE SCHOOLER

P.O. Box 35007, Colorado Springs, Colorado 80935

Library of Congress Catalog Card Number: 94-49057
ISBN 08910-98682

Cover design: David Shultz/Shultz Design & Advertising

Some of the anecdotal illustrations in this book are true
to life and are included with the permission of the persons
involved. All other illustrations are composites of real situations, and any resemblance to people living or dead is
coincidental.

Schooler, Jayne E.
    Searching for a past : the adopted adult's unique
process of finding identity / Jayne Schooler.
        p.   cm.
    Includes bibliographical references.
    ISBN 0-89109-868-2
    1. Adoptees—United States—Identification.
2. Adoptees—United States—Identification—Case
studies.   3. Birthparents—United States—Identification.   4. Birthparents—United States—Identification
—Case Studies.   I. Title.
HV875.55.S36   1995
362.8—dc20   94-49057
                                          CIP

Printed in the United States of America

1 2 3 4 5 6 7 8 9 10 11 12 13 14 15/00 99 98 97 96 95

CONTENTS

Dedicated to the memory of
Grace M. Ginter
1944–1993
A special friend, an insightful adoptive parent, a portrait of grace
She loved unconditionally

ACKNOWLEDGMENTS

Just as with my first experience in writing a book, I have again been reminded that no project of this nature is attempted without support and the help of others. It is truly impossible to thank each one who touched this project in some way. However, I would like to express my deep appreciation to the following:

To Betsie Norris, whose incredible insight and contributions brought about the reality of this book. Betsie is an inspiration and strength to those who meet her. Following the successful conclusion of her own search, Betsie did not forget the many who walked behind her. She stopped, turned around, saw a need, and moved to meet it. Betsie, with the assistance of others, established the Adoption Network Cleveland, a support and advocacy group in 1988. Betsie is a psychiatric nurse on a pediatric unit in a hospital in Cleveland, but still volunteers over forty hours a week of her time to help others find answers to the very same questions she herself once had. Betsie, once a seeker, is now a helper. One doesn't often meet someone with such character qualities as she possesses. Thank you, Betsie.

To my editor, Traci Mullins, who is always an encourager and to Nancy Burke, editorial assistant, who is always readily available to answer questions.

To the scores of adult adoptees from around this country who shared their stories, their successes, and their pain.

To Judy Johnson, a good friend, whose honest critiques smoothed out many rough spots, and to Diane Zodikoff for research assistance.

To Sarah Bethune, for invaluable research assistance and for sharing a part of her journey with me.

To Karen Reed, who traveled over many miles with me sharing the unfolding of this book

To the following professionals who took time out of extremely busy schedules for interviews and chapter critiques: Dirck Brown, Kate Burke, Bonnie Carroll, Susan Cox, Ronnie Diamond, Susan Freivalds, Marian Parker, Joyce Maguire Pavao, Sharon Kaplan Roszia, Randolph Severson, Anu Sharma, Nancy Ward, Linda Yellin, Kay Donley Zeigler.

To Ohio Search and Support Groups: Reunite in Columbus (Kathy Singer and Becky Hall), Chosen Children in Dayton, and Adoption Network Cleveland.

To my colleagues at Warren County Children's Services, Lebanon, Ohio, and a special thank-you to Mr. R. D. Burchwell, Executive Director and Placement Supervisor, and Mr. Steve Kelhoffer for their patience and flexibility in allowing me time to work on this project.

To the constant encouragers: Celina Meyer, Linda Smith, Jackie Wright, Pat Cobb, Pam Handley, Betsy Bingham, Joe Atkinson, Patti Jacobs, Lavonne Dursch, and scores of friends from the West Carrollton (Ohio) Nazarene Church.

To my husband, David, son, Ray, and daughter, Kristy, for their always present support.

Finally, I am deeply grateful to God for opening doors to new experiences, for bringing the right people to me at just the right time, and for the strength and insight needed to complete this project.

Adoption—
From the
Other Side of
Childhood

❖

CHAPTER ONE

GROWING UP ADOPTED: THE UNIQUE STRUGGLES

———— ✤ ————

I remember thinking when I was

young that I must have come into

this family because it was where I

was supposed to be. My sense of loss

came about mostly because of the

secrecy. I wondered what was so bad

about me and my background that I

wasn't allowed to know about it.

BETSIE NORRIS

Born with brilliant red hair and a spunky personality to match, Betsie Norris joined her adoptive family when she was sixteen days old. Betsie always knew about her adoption. Reared by loving parents who understood the need to communicate with her about it, Betsie grew up feeling comfortable with the relationship. Yet within this positive, open environment, adoption still sent her on an intensely emotional journey, a fragile search for people in her past she did not know.

Also adopted as an infant, Sue McDonald grew up in an adoptive home that emphasized her "chosenness," her "specialness." She knew her parents loved her and she felt intensely loyal to them. She kept the reality of adoption tucked away until early adulthood. Following the death of her parents, Sue felt free to begin her journey, to confront the intensity of her losses. She needed to find an understanding of feelings she didn't comprehend. Ultimately she made a decision not to search.

Adopted as an older child at age seven, Nancy Grower was separated first from her birth family and then tragically from a younger brother who had come with her to a children's home. Nancy entered a home environment where adoption talk was strictly forbidden, her name changed to erase her past, and her feelings forced underground. Adoption set Nancy on a walk to face an indistinct past, to reconnect with those who were faint within her memory.

Making plans for an overseas trip, Robert Walker began collecting the needed documentation for his passport. Officials at the state vital statistics department couldn't locate the most obvious one, his birth certificate. Confused, he casually mentioned the dilemma to his father whose reaction was startling. As his father stumbled around for a plausible explanation, it became apparent to Robert that a significant problem existed.

Robert's father finally told him the truth: He was adopted. Learning this at age thirty-four sent Robert on a path strewn with uncertainty, mistrust, and secrecy. Each step felt like quicksand as he attempted to discover hidden truths and find answers to questions he never would have thought to ask. The journey would reshape his life with a new meaning that seemed fleeting, unreal, and ill-defined.

Betsie, Sue, Nancy, and Robert represent a broad spectrum of the millions of adults who have grown up in adoptive homes. Some entered those homes as infants, others as older children. Some experienced openness and communication about their past, others encountered blank looks and raised eyebrows as hushed tones squelched their normal curiosity. A few stumbled into the "secret" of their adoptive status while in late adolescence, even adulthood, finding themselves bewildered and confused. For most, their adoption experience created questions to be answered, a past to be found, and deep-seated emotional issues to be resolved. In essence, a life-long process, unique to each person, in an attempt to find Self.

GROWING UP ADOPTED

Many adopted persons who were children in the fifties, sixties, and seventies felt as if they grew up under the shadow of secrecy, silence, and in some cases, shame. Others found their adoptive experience to be open, positive, warm, and fulfilling.

Cindy Lafferty, adopted from a children's home in 1954, recalls her earliest memory of adoption.

"I was sitting in the back yard playing dolls with a neighbor girl. I was about eight years old. She told me something that day that I didn't at first believe.

"'Guess what? You're adopted. My mother told me so.'

"Startled by that revelation and not sure exactly what adoption meant, I went in to ask my mother. Hesitantly she told me that yes, I was adopted. She briefly told me a few details. She ended the conversation that day with, 'You're our little girl now; you don't need to think about this anymore.'"

At eight years of age Cindy received a message that adoption was to be kept a secret and forgotten. She also learned it was a topic that seemed to make people uncomfortable.

"If I was in a group of people and the opportunity to mention it came up, I did. Everyone would get quiet—they didn't know what to say. Some people joked about it because they didn't understand."

Unlike Cindy's experience of secrecy regarding adoption, Jennifer met with a total lack of communication on the subject. That silence created unsure footing for her as she entered her teen and young adult years and left her with a sense of shame.

Jennifer was adopted in 1963 as a two-year-old. She remembers being told of her adoptive status perhaps twice prior to her adolescence.

"No one ever mentioned the word *adoption* around me, so I couldn't ask anyone about it. By late elementary age, I knew I was different and adoption wasn't normal. I then began to wonder if adoption was bad."[1] That sense of shame followed Jennifer into a turbulent adolescence filled with low self-esteem and feelings of worthlessness.

The power of secrecy to disrupt positive emotional development can be seen in the life stories of many adoptees. Author and adult adoptee Robert Anderson said, "One does not build a house on a sandbar or a personality on a pile of problematic secrets. Feeling secure about oneself is difficult when basic aspects are unknown and frightening. It is all too easy to worry about what might be at the core of the secrets with the possibilities limited only by one's imagination."[2] For some, growing up adopted created memories filled with pain, disillusionment, and wonder. For others, the adoption experience brought positive emotional growth and fulfilling memories.

Dianne Bonecutter's adoption experience produced in her affirmative feelings. Learning of her adoption at age five, Dianne recalls warm memories throughout childhood.

"I had a little ironing board, and when my mom would iron clothes, I would iron my dolls' clothes while we talked. One of the neighbors was pregnant and I asked my mom what it had been like when she was pregnant with me. Without skipping a beat, she said, 'Well, I didn't have you; you were what is called adopted.'

"I never felt out of place growing up adopted. I always felt it was very special to be their chosen one. I felt lucky being adopted into this family. They always accepted me as the adopted one but never referred to me as such. I was never given anything but love and respect and a sense of belonging."

Betsie, who grew up the only girl along with two adopted brothers, felt content with her adoptive status. "Adoption was such a normal thing in our family and my parents handled it so well." Yet, in spite of the family's openness of communication regarding adoption issues, Betsie still dealt with some issues. "I felt different because I didn't look like the others," she commented. "I had no real conscious feeling of being different. But looking back now as an adult, I think I felt it more than I realized."

According to Michigan therapist and adult adoptee, Linda Yellin, "When one is adopted, no matter how accepting, loving, or nurturing the adoptive parents are, consciously or unconsciously there is still a blow to one's self-esteem as a result of not being kept."[3] Some, if not all, issues for adopted persons begin with a sense of abandonment and rejection. From that grow other issues that confront adoptees throughout life as they put adoption within the context of their life history.

CORE ISSUES FOR ADOPTED PERSONS

For some, the question "Why did my parents give me away?" is no more than a passing thought. For others it is an obsession that can't be stilled.

Linda sees this common thread in her clinical work with adopted persons.

Many adoptees struggle with integrating their intellectual understanding of the facts and the societal norms at the time of their release with the feelings that come with the question "Why was I given away?" They remain emotionally confused. It is more than just feeling unwanted, but wondering how anyone could give away flesh and blood. They are puzzled why no one would help the birth mother. They want to know what's behind the real story.

As adopted persons encounter adoption issues, whether in early or mid-adolescence (or for the first time in adulthood), this confusion leads them to deal with what many experts feel is the hub around which all other adoption issues revolve.

Loss

Around the age of ten or eleven, I really began to understand what adoption meant—I had gained a family. I soon came to realize something else—I had also lost a family in the process. Where is that family now?
—John Bakosh, age 28

I think I felt the losses in my life when I found my birth family. I had wonderful adoptive parents but grew up an only child. I didn't know my birth situation, so I wasn't sure if I had siblings. I had a strong inner feeling that I did. When I found out I had four brothers and sisters, all I could think about were the tragically lost years without them.
—Marsha Hollinger, age 37

Adoption is the only relationship in life that by its very existence creates loss for everyone involved. "Without loss, there would be no adoption. Loss is the hub of the wheel."[4] All those within the adoption triad—birth parents, adoptive parents, and adopted child—have experienced at least one life-changing loss.

For many adoptive parents that loss is created by infertility. A portion of those losses include loss of a biological child, loss of dreams for a family as planned, loss of status as biological parents, and loss of providing grandparents with a biological child.[5]

For the birth parents, that loss includes the lifelong relationship with their birth child and all the other painful issues attached to that.

15

For the adopted child, the list is a long one. "The adoptee experiences many losses over a lifetime: loss of birthparents, loss of a biological connection to the adoptive parents, the loss of status as a normal member of society with one father and one mother, the loss of birth family ties, loss of cultural heritage, loss of siblings, loss of genetic information."[6] For all affected by adoption, "it is these losses and the way they are accepted and hopefully resolved that set the tone for the lifelong process of adoption."[7]

For some the loss feels like an amputation that leaves them vulnerable to future losses. As she grew older and moved into her mid-thirties, Sue McDonald encountered for the first time a profound sense of what she didn't have. She now knows that as a young person, she kept adoption issues hidden well below ground.

"Before I had my daughter, much of my adoption stuff was underground for me. When she was born, it really hit me that to my knowledge, she was the only connection in blood that I had. I was unprepared for the intense feeling of loss I experienced and still do."

Challenged with new feelings and emotional experiences at the birth of her daughter, Sue recognized she was dealing with a pervasive feeling of disconnectedness in her life. After she experienced a strong bond to her daughter, she understood for the first time what connectedness felt like. Not only did she feel disconnectedness as a loss, Sue also commented that the secrecy of her adoption left her without a history, without life in its truest context—her own reality. Her journey into the pain of loss is bringing some resolution.

Anderson, in the book *Second Choice*, comments about loss: "Life consists of a series of losses, which by themselves do not cause psychopathology. One does better to confront a loss directly; ignoring it or wrapping it with platitudes may obviate the need for grief over the short term, but invites a problem with self-esteem over the long term."[8]

In *Faces of Rage*, author David Damico says that if we fail to resolve loss in a healthy manner, it could have the following consequences:

- We will impair our ability to recognize and comfort others in pain.
- We will injure our ability to feel and remember as our practice of blocking out bad times extends to difficulty in remembering good times as well.
- We will force ourselves into self-protection that will keep others at arm's length.
- We will project our own fears and beliefs into our present moments.

- ◆ We will construct walls of rage that lock the needy part of ourselves inside away from anyone—including God—who can heal and restore us.

"Unresolved loss," warns Damico, "extends to every aspect of our physical, emotional, and spiritual being."[9]

For some adopted persons, resolution of the loss has carried them through much emotional work. Damico offers encouraging insight into this journey of loss resolution:

> When we allow ourselves to experience pain, hope begins to enter. It reminds us of the loss, which always hurts. But the reminder of the loss helps us clear a path through the pain to a new shore. When we get there we will be different—so will our world. Hope brings us to acceptance. Never ignoring or erasing the loss or pain, hope teaches us to respond to and honor loss. It brings dignity to pain. It makes us strong, more authentic, and more understanding of others whose losses mirror ours.[10]

For those who are still continuing the journey through loss or have touched a point of resolution, another issue may silently clamor for recognition.

Abandonment and Rejection

Throughout my entire life, I always heard the "your mother loved you so much, she gave you to us" story. It never made much sense to me. Reality is, she left me.
—Robert Sawyer, age 26

I have always wondered what I could have done to force my mother to get rid of me. Maybe if I hadn't cried so much.
—Katie Johnson, age 21

I grew up with the fear that some day I was going to wake up and nobody would be there. The house would be empty. They would have all disappeared. Maybe that's what happened to me in the very beginning.
—Kim Kelly, age 28

The word *reject* means "to repel, to repudiate, to throw back or throw out as useless or substandard." A large shadow looming over the lives of many adopted persons is the feeling of being rejected. Rehearsing rejection and abandonment, for some, becomes a way of managing the pain.

Rejection must rank as one of life's most anguishing experiences. Especially in the vulnerable years of adolescence into early adulthood, feelings of rejection on the part of the adopted person can override the positive and nurturing love given to them by their adoptive parents. Their perceptions of rejection can spill over to affect the building of healthy relationships. Some develop patterns of pursuing acceptance but then back away when emotional intimacy gets too close.

Cathy, the beautiful twenty-two-year-old daughter of Robert and Donna Rider, would enthusiastically call her mom and dad from college to report on her newest romantic prospect. But after a few dates, Cathy began refusing invitations to go out. Her roommates told her parents that she never went out with the same boy for very long at all. Her behavior stumped her parents.

Cathy's evasive behavior is typical of a person dealing with rejection issues. Cathy was adopted by the Riders when she was a month old. Their openness about how she was separated from her family gave her answers to the facts, but she repeatedly asked questions they couldn't answer. "Why did they get rid of me? Why did they leave?" Cathy's perception of rejection was so strong that in most of her relationships she rebuffed girlfriends and boyfriends before they rejected her.

In an attempt to come to an understanding of the issue of abandonment and rejection, Sharon Kaplan-Roszia suggests questions an adopted person can ask to sort through the pain.

- How has rejection played a role in my life in response to loss?
- Have I become a people-pleaser to feel accepted? or am I an extremely angry, rejecting person?
- Have I caused significant others to reject me over time because of those initial losses in adoption?[11]

A final question: What will I now do with this perception of rejection?

As adoptees get in touch with feelings of loss, rejection, and abandonment, other sensitivities may emerge that touch deep chords of self-worth.

Shame and Guilt

I knew my birth mother was only seventeen when I was born. When I was growing up, if I did something really wrong, my father would ask, "Are you going to be like your mother?" I lived under such a shadow; if

they thought she was so bad, I must be too.
—Gloria McFarland, age 29

I could never talk about adoption in our house. If I brought it up, you would have thought I'd said a dirty word. I grew up thinking that because adoption was a bad word, there was something terribly wrong with me.
—Jackie Bauer, age 33

Whenever I acted up, my mother would go into a lecture: Don't you appreciate what we have done for you? I felt guilty all the time for failing to act like they wanted me to.
—David Walker, age 24

"It is a very heavy feeling, this pervasive sense of shame. It is the ongoing premise that one is fundamentally bad, inadequate, defective, unworthy, or not fully valid as a human being."[12]

The feeling of shame is not about what we did or did not do. It is about our very selves. It is about who we are. Shame tells us we are unworthy, horribly unworthy. "Shame is without parallel—a sickness of the soul."[13]

Adoption exposes a person to this invisible sense of shame. Why? Because the most conspicuous way for a parent to create shame within a child is to turn his back upon him, to fail to take responsibility for him, according to Lewis Smedes in his book, *Shame and Grace: Healing the Shame We Don't Deserve.* Adoption, by its mode of creation, constructs this perception within a child that translates into shame.

Kristy, twenty-three, felt disowned by her birth mother, the woman who gave her life and then gave her away. Kristy knew intellectually that having been given up for adoption as a baby had absolutely nothing to do with her as a person. However, it was not what she thought that drove her spirit but what she felt. Her feelings told her that if she had been worth it, her mother would have moved mountains to keep her.

Another source of shame for many adopted adults is the feeling that they never were what their adoptive parents had hoped for. They never measured up to the child their parents could not conceive. This left them with the awesome pain of not only never "being" that dreamed-for child, but never "doing" the right thing.

Guilt for the adoptee is rooted not only in a sense of never doing the right thing—never measuring up within the adoptive home—but in feeling that even as a small child she or he caused the break-up of the relationship within the birth family.

For Nancy Gower, that feeling of guilt followed her throughout childhood. "I never really felt like I fit in, and I always wondered why I was taken away. What had *I* done wrong?"

Feelings of guilt and shame overlap. They are fluid feelings that never stay in their own place quite the way our labels want them too.[14] One feels guilty for something he has done, and he feels shame for being the type of person who would have done it.

As an adult, facing feelings of shame can be a freeing experience. Smedes suggests three discoveries a person can make about himself:

- ♦ I am someone to whom someone made an unconditional commitment from the beginning.
- ♦ I am someone whose parents consider me worthy of the love they give.
- ♦ I have the power to own myself: I take responsibility for my life, I am proud to be who I am, and I have joy in being myself.[15]

Core issues such as loss, rejection, shame, and guilt often confront adoptees as they face gnawing emotional pain. Another core issue usually wells up in adolescence and seeks resolution well into adulthood.

Identity
"Who am I?" "Who do I look like?" "Who do I act like?" These questions are wrapped up in identity formation. Getting information about their birth families quells the issue for those adoptees who can integrate their two identities. For others, it can lead to more confusion because of the vast differences between the adoptive family and birth family.

"Most adoptees feel an extreme sense of sadness, pain, and confusion," says Joseph Soll of New York, an adoptee and psychotherapist. "There's a sense of unreality, of not being born properly. Not being real. Not being a part of society."[16]

What does a problem with identity feel like?

Feeling Different
Kim, a twenty-five-year-old adopted woman from Korea, almost daily encountered a feeling of being different.

"When we went to a restaurant, grocery store, just about anywhere, I could sense people turning their heads to look at us. I knew they were won-

20

dering where I came from. I was born in Korea and it's obvious that I'm adopted."

Penny also grew up with a feeling of being different, wondering who she was and where she fit in. When she joined her family at the age of two, she was the only child. Soon to follow would be three children born to her adoptive parents. She grew up in a loving, nurturing family of very light-complexioned blonds. Her two sisters and brothers all towered over her in height. She felt like the only "short and fat" one in the house. Her own perceptions of these major differences created a sense of confused identity— "Who am I really? I don't fit here."

Something Is Missing

"People ask me, 'Don't you hate your mother?' 'No,'" says Nanci Hubsch. "How could I ever hate somebody I don't know? How could I love somebody I don't know? I just have a million questions: Did you ever think about me? Did you ever try to find me? Were you ever curious about how I grew up?

"My adoptive parents are my parents—I love them to death and I don't want to hurt them. But I've always had the feeling that something was missing. I don't know how to explain it. It wasn't anything my (adoptive) parents did wrong. It's just something that's always been there." [17]

Carole Wallenfelsz, an adoptee experienced the same feelings. "I love my parents dearly. They raised me with good moral values, a sense of family, and a lot of love. But still, I needed to meet the woman who gave birth to me. As much of a cliché as it may seem, I needed to find that missing puzzle piece." [18]

In moving toward resolution of the issue of identity, Carole discovered a secret.

"Much of my adolescence was a furious search for identity, natural for that age, but was intensified by my preoccupation—almost an obsession— with being adopted. As I grew older I grew calmer. The obsession dwindled to a desire. I learned that my identity was what I made myself. I started to define myself based on me, not on what might have been if only I had known my birth mother." [19]

WISE ADVICE

Listening to those who now view adoption from the other side of childhood offers an opportunity to improve the experience for all whose lives are touched by the experience. What advice do these adults give?

If I could change something, it would be that I was told sooner and that I felt free to talk about it.
—Julie White, age 42 (She found out by accident at the age of fourteen that she was adopted.)

I wish I could change how my parents understand my need and desire to know the truth. I don't want to hurt them. It's about me, not them.
—Thomas Ward, age 38

We were taken from our parents when I was around seven. I wish my adoptive parents would have communicated with me and given me reasons for what happened. I wish my brother and I had not been separated. I had cared for him but I was never permitted to see him. I also wish that someone would have guided me through the whole experience from day one of separation from my birth family.
—Nancy Grower, age 56

If I could change something, it would be that my parents hadn't so emphasized their view of what was positive—that I had been "chosen"—rescued almost. I would like to have been allowed to talk about some of the negatives—like feeling so different from them.
—Sue McDonald, age 45

I love my adoptive parents and I'm grateful I had the opportunity to be raised by them, but that doesn't make me grateful I was given up for adoption. I can't say it would have been better this way or that way. I do think it helped contribute an aspect to my personality that maybe, otherwise, would not have been there. I think adoptees have to be flexible and perceptive to grow up in a family they are not biologically connected to. We have to figure things out as we go along. I don't think we know internally what the rules or standards are as much as someone intricately connected biologically.
—Betsie Norris, age 34

Growing up adopted, for many persons, sets them on a peculiar and unique journey as they begin to put their lives in perspective. It's a journey to discover something about themselves—a journey to reconnect a broken cord. It's a journey to embrace what one has been given, to grieve what one has lost, and to build upon what one has discovered.

CHAPTER TWO

TO SEARCH
OR NOT TO SEARCH

---◈---

I recall the times I thought of calling

the agency where I was adopted for

information. I looked up the number

in the phone book numerous times,

but the guilt was overwhelming.

I felt social workers would not

understand; they would think I was

ungrateful. How dare I want

to know my own medical history,

what my parents looked like, or why

they placed me for adoption.[1]

BETSIE NORRIS

As she rounded the corner, her eye caught a glimpse of the house. It was an average-sized house, neatly kept, with a row of rose bushes lining the driveway. *Roses,* Jackie thought to herself, *she likes roses, too.*

Nearing the front sidewalk, she slowed her step. A rising sense of anxiety gripped her. She almost wished she hadn't taken it this far, but she couldn't quell the ache in her heart. A letter had been the first step. Then the phone calls. Now Jackie would soon face the woman who gave her birth. *What will she think of me?* she wondered.

Today marked the end of Jackie's two-year search for the only person she hoped had all the answers to her questions. The search and reunion was something she had to do.

Ellen, Jackie's younger sister, understood Jackie's need to find her birth mother. She freely encouraged Jackie through the search process, but it wasn't an important issue for Ellen. Possibly someday. Maybe never. It just wasn't something she had to do.

To search or not to search? Each year, thousands of adult adopted persons ask and answer this question. Perhaps you're asking it now.

What is the meaning of the search? Why do some search just for information and stop? Why do some seek a reunion? Why do some wait until mid-life while others choose to do nothing? Is there a right time to search? What advice can be given to those in the decision-making stage? All these questions deserve examination.

THE MEANING OF THE WORD *SEARCH*

When the word *search* is mentioned within the context of adoption, a picture emerges in one's mind. Captured within the frame of that picture is a young man or young woman sitting at a courthouse backroom table pouring over dusty, yellowed files. From the intense facial expression, one senses the emotional urgency to catch just a glimpse of his or her unknown past.

The word *search* for an adopted person carries with it multiple layers of meaning. For some, "searching" means attempting to find nonidentifying information about birth parents' characteristics or one's own medical history with no attempt for a meeting.

For others, *search* means reunion—a face-to-face meeting. For still more adoptees, the meaning and process move them profoundly deeper. The word *search* for many is not limited to its literal meaning of a physical effort to make a connection. The meaning expands to include all that is part of the adoptee's quest, for it is an emotional, psychological, and spiritual quest.

Randolph Severson, in an eloquent explanation of all that resides within the quest, said the following:

> Perhaps every adoptee bears within himself the imprint of a special or unique spiritual vocation. It is spiritual. It is always spiritual . . . the matter of the heart and soul. . . . The mystery of adoption is that the adoptee was truly, as Betty Jean Lifton has said, twice born . . . born first of the flesh and then again in the spirit.
>
> If an adoptive family is anything, it is a spiritual, psychological reality whose ground is love. What's an adoptive family made of if not biology and genes. Heart and soul can be the only answer.
>
> To be adopted then, is to be both born of the heart and born of the spirit. The life work of the adoptee, if he or she is to attain healing and wholeness is to rejoin the heritage of the flesh and the beauties of the spirit within the secret treasuring of the heart.[2]

WHY ADOPTEES SEARCH

Robert Anderson, in his article, "Why Adoptees Search—Motivations and More," asks simple yet profound questions.

"This question, I believe, why adoptees search, can be paraphrased, 'Why are you interested in your mother, your father, your grandparents, sisters, brothers, cousins, nephews, ancestry, history, aptitudes? In short, why are you interested in you?'"[3]

The Search As an Adventure

Anderson, from his view as an adopted person and psychiatrist, says he believes people search for a number of reasons. First, they search as an adventure. Often viewed as an exciting undertaking, it is an effort on the part of the adoptee to move life to a new vantage point, to fill in the missing gaps, and to clutch the time that remains with family members previously unknown. It is an effort uncomplicated by contemplating how the reunion will alter the lives of all those touched by the course of events.

Adoption therapist, Sharon Kaplan-Roszia commented that some people, by temperament, are natural mystery solvers. Throughout life they have processed people and events, solved problems, unraveled mysteries. Being curious is simply part of their nature. So to search, she said, is the most natural thing for them to do.[4]

For those who search as an adventure, Anderson says, it becomes a "drama of individuals prevailing against great odds to finally be reunited with their biological families. It can be of heroic proportion, and it may intimate that the characters should be rewarded for their efforts, perhaps by thereafter having a joyous life together."[5]

The Search as Therapy

For most adoptees, facing the issue of the search is far more than "just an adventure." It is often a frightening decision, filled with enormous physical and emotional investment. It often comes after years of pondering, waiting for the courage to begin. It is a therapeutic step because it confronts facts, issues, people, and feelings that were once vague wonderings. It brings most to a point of resolution regarding the complexities of growing up as an adopted child. The result of the search spans a wide continuum for each adopted person, from satisfying a need for factual information to touching the deepest level of the heart and soul with a reunion.

I'm Not Who I Thought I Was: What Is My Real Medical History?

Learning of her adoption at the age of forty-four sent Jan Campbell on an unsettling investigation. Regrouping emotionally from the most traumatic disclosure of her life, Jan wanted to know her birth family's medical history. The answers brought a profound change in her perspective about her future.

> Initially, the main reason I searched was to find my medical history. I assumed that my (adoptive) mother's medical history was mine; she had died at forty-two of a heart attack. Her parents also died very young—in their early sixties. I was very concerned about my health, preoccupied is probably a better word, from the time I was first married on. I wondered if I would live to see my children to adulthood. It came as a great relief to discover that my adoptive mother's medical history was *not mine*, and now I wanted to know what my actual medical history was.

Do I Look Like Anyone? Do I Act Like Anyone?

When Penny, a thirty-year-old with auburn hair and freckles, decided to search, her intent was to gather only information. Throughout her teens and early adulthood, Penny felt frustrated, embarrassed, and insecure because she looked so unlike anyone in her adoptive home. The driving desire to find a genetic similarity was the only thing that encouraged Penny during the ten months it took to receive information:

> For the first time in my life, I felt physically attached to someone.

The information I received told me that I look like both my birth father and birth mother, suffer with her allergies, and now I understand why I have such an interest in music. They both did. My reason for the search was not to hurt my relationship with my adoptive parents. I just wanted to know who I looked like and who I acted like. At this point in my life, I am not ready to meet them. Maybe someday. Right now, I am able to put the compelling search effort to rest.[6]

The Emptiness in My Heart Wouldn't Go Away

A common theme for many adopted persons is gratitude for their adoptive parents and how they handled adoption issues. To them, their parents did everything right, but it was still not enough. For Marla Van Wassenhove, it was a need that even she didn't recognize until her adoptive parents touched the right chord. She says:

> Even though I had a wonderful life and great parents, I was down a lot and felt empty inside. I felt I didn't know who I was or where I came from. I just didn't feel whole. My parents could see I was hurting, even when I couldn't see it myself. They talked to me about this and we decided to search.

Sandy Garfield experienced a similar positive home environment to Marla's but found out by age thirty that the hushed but ever-present pain of her heart could no longer be stilled.

> I always wanted to know facts about my adoption, but by the time I reached thirty, the need was far deeper . . . I had significant questions to ask. Why was I given away? The only way I could put the pieces of my life together was to find the pieces myself. I waited as long as I could until the anguish became unbearable. I needed answers from those who, hopefully, had held me even for just a moment before saying goodbye.

A Life Transition Brought Me Face to Face with My Adoption

For many adoptees, the decision to search emerges following a significant transitional event such as marriage, the birth of a child—giving the searcher the first contact with a blood relative—or the death of an adopted family member.

"When adoptive parents die," said Dr. David Brodzinksy, "the adoptee might suddenly feel compelled to put a name and face to the phantom 'other' parents who had been companions of his childhood fantasies. . . . Since the unconscious knows no time barriers, losses tend to pile up, and the most recent loss drives the adoptee to resolve the first loss, the one that remains potentially reversible."[7] For one young adult, this proved to be true.

Dealing with adoption issues was something that thirty-one-year-old Tina Stephenson ignored throughout her life. From an early age she stuffed thoughts and feelings away about being adopted. As an adult she found herself standing face to face with old feelings left over from childhood.

"In my heart I wanted to belong to my mom and dad," Tina said. "I wanted to be their biological child. I was embarrassed that I was adopted, and I felt that if people knew I wasn't really a "Wheeler," they might think differently of me."

Tina's confrontation of the reality of her adoption is quite similar to some adult adoptees. Some face it early and look for answers in their late teens. Still others, like Tina, do not face it until a major life transition looms before them. For Tina, it was the death of her adoptive mother that brought her adoption issues to the surface.

"Overnight it hit me. Somewhere out there is someone who looks like me," she exclaimed. Following the death of her adoptive mother, the reality of another person distantly tied to her life emerged. After nearly thirty years, Tina faced the reality of her adoption and the implications that came with it. She initiated a search to find out as much about her birth family as possible.

With the help of her supportive husband, David, Tina set out on a journey to locate her birth parents. Unfortunately for Tina, the need to connect was not mutual. Her birth mother, up to this point, has rejected any effort on Tina's part to meet. Any path to locate her birth father is also blocked. Tina's need to stand face to face with her birth family is a continual one. She simply wants to finish developing a picture that was exposed at the time of her adoptive mother's death.[8]

It Was a Question That Has Always Been with Me

Actually making a decision to search, for many adopted persons, is a resolve made even before adolescence. One adoptee commented, "I started my search probably from the first time I realized what 'adopted' meant. I think every adopted person searches, if only in their minds. If they are like me, they searched in the quiet darkness of their bedroom late at night. They searched by asking themselves questions no one was around to hear— questions no one could criticize, analyze, or judge."

Susan Friel-Williams was one of those lifetime searchers.

The decision to search was not something I made a conscious decision to start. I just knew that someday I was going to need the answers. I guess the first time I thought about it was when I was twelve. I had always wondered who I looked like and why I was so different from my family. I was the only blond in a family of brunettes. I am left-handed. I am artistic, both art-wise and musically.

A family member who knew my birth father told me his name when I was twelve. His name, which was a very long, difficult ethnic name, burned itself across my memory like a laser beam. I knew even at twelve that it was important and that I could *not* forget it.

I Needed to Connect with My Roots

Stemming from one of adoption's major issues—loss—many adopted adults initiate their search from a deep, pervasive feeling of disconnectedness, of having a piece of themselves missing and incomplete. There is a need, as mentioned by Dr. Randolph Severson, to "rejoin the heritage of the flesh and the beauties of the spirit within the secret treasuring of the heart."[9] It is a compelling necessity to meet the people who brought them life.

For Betsie Norris, growing up in a warm, nurturing adoptive home that gave her the message, "talking about adoption in this house is okay," still left loose ends. The sense of disconnectedness followed at her heels. She comments about her struggle.

Where did I get my red hair? What nationality am I? These were questions I faced daily. I also knew nothing about my birth. Was it an easy or difficult labor? What time was I born; how much did I weigh? Where was I for two weeks before placement? Deeper inside me were more questions. What kind of body was I growing into? How did my birth mother feel about me—then and now? Did she think of me? Why was I given up? That was the biggest question.[10]

In order to connect the scattered pieces of her life, the only thing for Betsie to do was make the decision to find her birth parents.

As I grew up, I always knew I would search, but I never pictured it as real or as potentially leading to a reunion. Adoption was steeped in unreality and disconnectedness engendered by the closed system mentality. I got the message to pretend adoption did not make a difference, that my family was like any other family. Part of me felt like an alien alone in the world. I felt ruled by fate not knowing who I was; therefore, not knowing what I could do in life. Later I heard terms like "biological alien" and "genealogical bewilderment" which described how I felt.[11]

For those who make a decision to locate birth family members, there are no promises as to the outcome. It could prove to be the most significant, positive event of one's life. It could also be a devastating blow to an already fragile self-esteem. In recent years, some adoption search groups have followed reunion results. A group in Canada, Parent Finders of Canada, surveyed five hundred members about their reunion experience. Here are the results they found:

SEARCHER	REUNITED WITH	FAVORABLE
Adoptee	Birth parent	92.0%
Adoptee	Birth Siblings	98.3%
Male Adoptee	Birth parent	92.6%
Male Adoptee	Birth siblings	100.0%
Female Adoptee	Birth parent	91.4%
Female Adoptee	Birth siblings	97.8%
Birth parents	Surrendered children	94.0%[12]

Many adults make a decision to search for a variety of reasons. However, there are reasons why some do not make the same decision.

Why Some Don't Search

Why some individuals decide not to search appears to be related to a variety of causes. Researchers in the field cite the following rationale for not conducting a search:

- ◆ Not interested right now
- ◆ Loyalty to adoptive parents
- ◆ Carrying other issues
- ◆ Uncertain about the right to disrupt lives
- ◆ Fear of rejection

I Am Just Not Interested Right Now
Sharon Kaplan-Roszia commented that some are just not interested. "Their

lives are full and busy with families or careers. Identity is not an issue for them," she added, "and it is something they don't want to do."[13]

For June Cannon, an adoptee in her thirties and also an adoption therapist, undertaking a search is not an important issue to her.

> My adoptive mom has always encouraged me to look, especially after my son was born. She thought the medical information would be helpful. But I just don't plan to at this point in my life for a number of reasons. First, I feel I have a pretty strong identity. This comes, I think, from the basic personality with which I was born. I feel confident and comfortable with myself. Second, I look like both my brother, who is also adopted, and my mom. I've heard that all my life.
>
> Another reason for not searching is how I was raised. I have never felt I was missing a piece of my life. My parents are dynamic people and I wanted to identify with them. They gave me security and a sense of belonging, but also a sense of autonomy. They would say, "Your accomplishments are yours"; they did not try to hold on to me too tightly.

I Feel a Strong Loyalty to My Adoptive Parents

At age twenty-six, Catherine McCally doesn't plan to search right now. She feels this decision is an outgrowth of her loyalty to her adoptive family— far outweighing a need for anything else.

Commenting about this conclusion, she said:

> I was placed with my family at four months. To this day we celebrate both my birthday and the anniversary of the day I was placed with my parents. I have a brother who is three years older than I am. He was adopted by my parents a year before me. He and I have discussed the idea of searching, but neither of us has had a desire to do so.
>
> I think the reason I'm not searching is that I don't have anything to search for. I have never felt anything was missing from my life. I am very close to both of my parents. I would not want to do anything to hurt them in any way. They are both older now. Maybe my feelings will change, but for now I'll leave the issue alone.

I Am Already in Too Much Pain

Julie White grew up in what she calls a dysfunctional family. Her adoptive status was not disclosed to her until the age of fourteen, and that was by accident. She has had a lifetime of discovering painful family secrets. Her anguish is evident as she shares.

> These last few years have been difficult. It has been a time of breaking silence about my father's alcoholism and dealing with "adult children of alcoholics" issues. I never really associated some of my emotional pain as being related to adoption, but I'm sure it is.
>
> Because mine was a private adoption where my family members knew my birth mother, the information is available to me. I'm not going to pursue it because I have an idealistic mind. I know that Marian and Richard, my birth parents, are "just people," and that's not good enough. I have unanswered questions and I don't suppose I'd like any of the answers. Also, I realize this woman is now in her sixties and we've managed to get this far without contact. Why should I create emotional upheaval for an older woman as well as for myself at mid-life? What gain could there be? I have already gone through the death of my dad, and my mom is seventy-four. I don't want to find a whole new family and face aging/death issues with them, too.

Do I Really Have the Right to Do This?

Some adopted persons, according to Sharon Kaplan-Roszia, have been given a message from society or from the family that wanting any information about their birth family is inappropriate or downright wrong. They may have grown up in a family where adoption talk was strictly avoided and they assumed the role of the grateful adoptee.[14]

At age twenty-seven, Nancy Kammer says that her need to find out anything about her birth family has caused turmoil throughout her adoptive family system. This turmoil created an emotionally complex tug-of-war for Nancy. She has yet to resolve the dilemma.

> Do I search for me . . . or do I not search for them? Can I handle what they will do if I decide to search? I've been told by my uncle, my aunt, and even my grandparents that what I want to do is upsetting my mom and dad. "Why can't I be grateful for what they have given me?" they ask. It makes me wonder if it's right for me to disrupt my adoptive parents' lives. It's very hard to want to pursue this search without feeling like I'm the one upsetting the otherwise peaceful boat.

I Can't Face Rejection—Again

While growing up, Sue McDonald kept her questions about her adoption deep inside herself. In mid-life, as she faced the meaning of adoption for her—that she had been given away—Sue lifted those fragile feelings from the backroom closet of her heart and confronted them. As a result, Sue made a decision not to search for any family members or for any information about herself.

> I can give you a long list of reasons why I am not searching. On the surface, they provide a great rationale for leaving the topic alone. First of all, I do not want to go through the process to find a family member dead and experience the grieving process for someone I don't know. Second, I don't want to take myself and my family on an incredible emotional roller coaster. Third, what will I do with what I find? I don't have an answer for that.

As Sue reflected on her reasons for choosing not to search, she reached deep into that hidden pain that had lain dormant for so long. "I have to admit, the main reason for leaving all of this alone is the terrible fear of rejection. I am continuing to work through what I feel as the consequence of my adoption. This emotional pain has impacted me so much that to risk more rejection is simply not worth it to me."

Adults who have taken the step to search have many positive reasons for the undertaking. For those who have decided not to search, the reasons need equal validation. To gain an objective perspective on the topic is to allow each individual to stand face to face with the question to search or not to search, for it is his decision alone. It is also necessary to allow time, maturity, and growth to complete its work and to rest with the conclusion at which the adopted person arrives. One young adoptee stated:

> *My birth mother made a decision many years ago to make an adoption plan for me. I was placed into a loving, warm family to whom I feel I belong. I appreciate my birth mother for her choice. I know she felt I could have a better life than what she could give to me. Yet I'm not ready to find her. Someday I will be ready.*
>
> *There are as many different answers to the question as there are people who contemplate it. It's a very curious thing, this process of search, for all adoptees at different times move along with different motivations. At some point we may be completely disinterested, almost apathetic about it. At another time in our lives each step may be fiercely compelled*

by the need to meet that person whose touch we may have felt but whose face we cannot remember.
—Heather Whitacre, age 25

Is There a Right Time to Search?

After weighing the views of those who have searched and those who have not, another step is advised. Before actually activating the search with the primary and hopeful outcome of reunion, it's important to assess your readiness. According to therapist Linda Yellin, there are several reasons why an adoptee may postpone his or her search to work on emotional readiness.

"One reason for waiting," states Yellin, "is that the adoptee searches with an absolute planned outcome and unrealistic expectations. These types of searchers are not prepared for the unexpected and are setting themselves up for more difficulty." Yellin believes that it's a normal part of the search process to have some fantasies, fears, hopes, and dreams about the birth family. Yet there are no guarantees about the outcome. Key questions to ask yourself are, "Am I ready for the unknown? Will I be okay no matter how it turns out?"

Another reason you should delay a search, according to Yellin, is that you may not be emotionally ready as a result of severe unmet needs in your adoptive family. "Searching for a birth parent or birth family with the hope of regaining a parent-child relationship with the birth family is unrealistic. Some grief work must be done around what was lost in the adoptive parent relationship and the birth parent relationship. Exploring some of the unmet needs will help move you toward more readiness."

A third argument for deferring the search, says Linda Yellin, is when it is not motivated by the adoptee, but by others pushing the issue. It's important for you to drive the search process. She adds, "From my firsthand experience as an adult adoptee who has searched and reunited, as well as from my involvement in the adoption community, the search and reunion process has been one of the most powerful experiences in my life. For the adoptees I have known, the search and reunion process provides opportunities for increased insight, strength, and healing and continues their journey of self-discovery as adults."

As Ken Burkett, a thirty-three-year-old adoptee who completed a search in 1993 expressed, "The search effort can be a great time of personal growth filled with discovery, pain, fulfillment, and healing. It is something the adoptee should only initiate himself when the time is right. It should never be another's decision."

Yellin believes that overall readiness to search occurs "when the adoptee wants to be in the driver's seat on the unknown search road of detours, bumps, roadblocks, rest stops, and curves in unpredictable weather."

Facing the decision to alter the relationships and events of your life and the lives of your birth family members, adoptive family members, and your own adult family is an important one. Listening to good advice in the early stages can bolster your courage to do what you feel you must.

ADVICE FROM SEARCHERS AND NON-SEARCHERS

The best advice I can think of is not to do it until you're sure you're emotionally ready for anything, like rejection or finding that maybe they do not meet your standards. You have to be ready to accept what you find no matter what it is and deal with it the best way you can. It's important to have someone in your corner like I did, helping you talk through things during your period of anticipation. My cousin and my husband were my rocks. Bear in mind that your birth family's personalities may be so different that you will have to do a lot of bending to try to understand or be understood, and most of all, do not push and do not judge.
—Dianne Bonecutter, age 42, reunited with birth family in 1993

Be infinitely patient. Be open to absolutely any response; things rarely turn out the way we fantasize. Honor your birth parents' right to privacy. Respect their decisions. Do not reveal who you are to any other family member inadvertently. Give your birth parents time.
—Jan Campbell, age 45, had contact with birth family members in 1993

Don't give up. If you truly want to find out, there are ways! The process is slow and frustrating. Sometimes you go down a dead-end street and don't know where to turn. If you have patience and determination, the pieces will slowly come together.
—Tina Stephenson, age 33, searched in 1993

As one who hasn't searched, I would say really think about it and think about why you are doing it! There is such a mix of positive and negative emotions regarding birth parents (or at least I feel such a mix) that I would need to be as sure as I could that I was searching for the good of all, not for some other need.
—Sue McDonald, age 45

There is no word in our language that adequately describes an adoptee's need to know his or her heritage. People refer to this need as "curiosity" as this is the closest term that seems to fit. The connotation of curiosity, however, is one of wanting to know for a potentially trivial reason. It does not describe the deep need to know experienced by many adoptees. I cannot imagine going through life not having searched, not having the opportunity to put the pieces of my life together.
—Betsie Norris, age 34, reunited with birth parents in 1986

Deciding to search does create a sense of ambivalence for adopted persons. Determining the whens, the hows, and the shoulds takes an immense amount of emotional energy. Perhaps the following poem readily expresses the dilemma of those facing a decision.

THE SHADOW FAMILY
Why do I fear you?
I have lived in your shadow
these years of my life.
I know you are there
    but where?
Show yourself—show yourself
    to me.
Please don't make me find you.
    Find me.
If I turn around fast, will I see you?
If I move my eyes there
    can I see you?
Do you have my eyes or
    are they mine?
Where is my smile—
    And my child's—
Are they yours?
I have pieces that don't match.
I have half-longings
and
Many years of half-cried tears.
                —Susan Kittel McDonald, 1990. Used by permission.

CHAPTER THREE

How to Communicate the Decision to Search to Your Adoptive Parents

✠

I did not want to hurt my adoptive

parents by my need to search.

Searching was something I had

to do for myself in order to be

a whole person.

BETSIE NORRIS

For the third time that evening, Robert laid the phone back on the receiver. He had planned to be at his parents' home for dinner within the hour and he now wanted to cancel. Until tonight he had avoided something he knew he had to do. He had brushed the issue aside for months. He didn't want to hurt them, but he needed to tell them about something he was thinking of doing. No, not just thinking about; he was doing it.

Tonight Robert would tell his parents that he had started a search for his birth parents. It was a search for answers—an exploration to find connections to the people who had given him life. It wasn't about them; they were wonderful parents. The search was about him. He had delayed as long as he could to share the search with them. He had waited until the unknowing became unbearable.

Communicating with adoptive parents and extended family members about the need to search presents a challenge for all adopted persons. For some, the challenge is minimal, the "telling" easy, the support present. For others, breaking silence about the people and circumstances that led to the formation of the adoptive family introduces a whirlwind of emotions that swirls around all parties touched by the opening of a previously closed, even taboo, issue.

Most adoptive parents agree that it's a natural thing for their adopted young person to want to know about his or her past. People need to know their roots. However, in responding to this need, feelings emerge that are considerably complex. For some parents, cognitive recognition that this is a normal issue for an adopted person stands miles apart from the psychological and emotional impact.

Randolph Severson, author and therapist, portrays the ambivalence encountered by some adoptive parents as they move toward honesty, enduring some confusion and even pain along the way.

> Adoptive parents—some with joy and some with anguish—are awakening to the fact that roots, however twisted, are as vital to the leafing of the tree as is the gentle nurturing of the sun and rain.[1]

Jill Gardner, an adopted person whose reunion is still in its infancy, encountered this dilemma with her parents. She commented, "Cognitively, my mom and dad were very supportive of my reunion. They said and did all the right things. However, emotionally my mom had a hard time. I overheard her talking on the phone. Her worst nightmare was that I would leave her for my biological mother. When we found my birth mother, my adoptive mother came face to face with her greatest fear. As it turned out, my relationship with my adoptive family has grown stronger."

Opening the door to discuss search and reunion issues with adoptive family members requires you to cross over what feels like a rickety, unstable bridge. That bridge, built by materials from an unknown past, reinforced by the circumstances of the present, yet jeopardized by the concealed issues of the future, stands shaky and uncertain.

As you near the bridge, you know that crossing it will alter the lives of everyone within your family circle. To gain support while crossing that span, you must take time to step into the shoes of those whose lives will be most greatly affected—your adoptive parents and grandparents. A step back into the last generation and a look into the future will provide helpful insight as you communicate with your family about your need to search and ask them for their blessing. How can that be done and what will it accomplish?

First, a glance back at the historical and societal attitudes present at the time of the adoption will help you recognize how the viewpoint of a generation ago shaped your parents' thinking and actions. Second, a look at the intergenerational changes that have occurred within your family's style of communication furnishes a unique insight into why parents perhaps failed to deal at all with adoption issues in the past two generations. Finally, listening to the feelings and deep concerns that fashion your parents' perception of their lifelong experience as adoptive parents will help you field their responses in the future as the search issues become an ever-increasing reality.

ADOPTION WITHIN AN HISTORICAL AND SOCIETAL CONTEXT

To facilitate good communication across the generations regarding the search and reunion issues, the adopted person must understand the generational context of both the institution of adoption and the perspective their adoptive parents and birth parents developed within that context.[2]
—Anu Sharma

From history's earliest days until the present, the practice of adoption has served a variety of functions, according to Kenneth Watson, Associate Director of Chicago Child Care Society. It has spanned a continuum of needs from "providing a royal family with an heir, to adding 'indentured' hands, to making a family financially self-sufficient, to emptying orphanages to save community dollars."[3]

In recent decades, adoption has served two additional functions—to meet the needs of couples whose dreams of a family were shattered by infertility and to provide a solution for birth parents who found themselves facing an unintended and untimely pregnancy.

What emerged from the latter two functions of adoption during the middle decades of this century was an idealistic picture, one which characterized a perfect solution to a societal problem. As Dr. Miriam Reitz, a family therapist, and Watson state:

> Adoptive families and adoption agencies collaborated to present adoption as what it can never really be—a chance for birth parents to go on happily with their lives, for children to grow up in trouble-free families, and for adoptive parents to fulfill themselves and find immortality through children to whom they have sole claim by virtue of adoption.[4]

What this "perfect solution" created were myths that were safeguarded throughout the adoption world.

"Years ago," according to Sharon Kaplan-Roszia, "myths were perpetuated through the adoption community. One myth taught those whose lives were touched by adoption that the most healthy attitude for all members of the triad was to make a clean break."[5] That break meant no looking back—for anyone, forever.

Growing up around that particular paradigm were other myths that fueled secrecy, forced denial and lies, and created unexpected heartbreaks.

We Did What We Were Told to Do

One primary attitude adoptive parents were told to assume following the finalization of the adoption was, "Take this child home, love him, and forget that he or she is adopted."

"Adoptive families were told to act just like biological families," Roszia commented. Birth certificates were amended to represent the adoptive parents as biological parents, a procedure some adopted persons now call "legal fiction." Parents were also told that secrecy is best for everyone. Those simple instructions played out in how parents handled the issues that were a part of their unique parenting experience.

We Kept It a Secret

When we brought Cathy home from the hospital, nearly thirty years ago, our social worker shared our excitement. She told us Cathy most likely would look like us, with her blond hair and blue eyes. No one would ever guess she was adopted. On the day of the court hearing, our worker said to us, "Now just take her home and love her like your own. Forget about the adoption. You are her only family."

So that's exactly what we did. In fact, we didn't tell Cathy about her adoption until she was nineteen. That was a horrible mistake. But we did what we were told to do.

—Sherry Brown, adoptive mother

For Sherry, her husband, Ken, and the hundreds of adoptive parents of the last generation, adoption was cast as merely an event in time—a static one, with no reference to the future. Many parents acted on the belief that there was no hidden agenda within adoption and that keeping the event a secret was the best approach. "Pretending" was promoted as the healthiest coping mechanism within the adoption community.

Watson remarked that "the implication of the adoption on the subsequent development of the child or the family was either viewed as inconsequential or denied altogether." These perceptions—"we are just like a biological family; adoption has no reference to the future, and things are best kept a secret"—further established a precedent on how children were told about their adoption, if they were told at all.

We Made Up a Story

We were advised by our agency to tell Ryan early on that he was adopted. We were also told, in order not to damage him with a negative story about his birth parents, to tell him they had both died in a car accident. We thought that was strange advice since we knew it wasn't true. Since our worker was the professional, we did what we were advised. It turned out to be very bad advice.

—David and Joanne West, adoptive parents

The Wests were not alone in the way they handled their son's adoption story. Many adoptive parents were directed to take that same route in order to protect a child's perception of his original family. The predicament for these parents was how to discuss adoption with the child in a way that gave them full entitlement as parents because they had "rescued" the child yet not paint a negative picture of the birth parents and do damage to the child's self-esteem.

It was not uncommon for adoptive parents, acting on the recommendation of their agency, to fabricate explanations for the circumstances of their child's birth and how they entered the family. Parents used a string of stories, from a range of freak accidents to unexplained disappearances, all done with the best intentions.

Parents were told to forget about the adoption, maybe not even mention it. They were instructed to deny any differences adoption might create within the family relationship and to fabricate stories about the adoption. Many parents were also handed another myth—"if they did a good job, their child would never wonder about his birth family. He would never want to search."

Exposing the Myth

Years ago, while sitting in the office of our agency worker, I asked her how to handle my son's curiosity about his birth family. I was told by her, "If you are the right kind of mother, your son will never want to search." The day Kevin came to me asking help in locating his birth mother sent me through a maze of guilt and inadequacy. How had we failed as parents? Our son wanted to find his birth family.
—Melanie Walker, adoptive parent

Carol Demuth, in her book *Courageous Blessing: Adoptive Parents and the Search*, says adoptive parents were given the message "If you were loving, nurturing parents who acknowledged your child's adoptive status early, there would be no need on his part to know anything else."

A Model of the Myth[6]		
What Parents Were	*Taught*	It'll be just like a biological family.
What Parents	*Understood*	Secrecy and fables are best.
What Parents	*Expected*	Child would never look back.
Parents Discovered	*Reality*	Many adoptees have missing pieces, feel empty, and must seek resolution.
Parents Experienced	*Frustration*	Issues of adoption and search are difficult to handle.
Parents Experienced	*Anger*	Someone didn't tell us the truth.
Parents Felt	*Betrayed*	Someone really lied to us.

Carol Demuth continues:

> Parents feel betrayed. Not by their child—but by the system that perpetuated a false image of what adoption could be. Parents were unfairly led to believe they could be everything to their children, that they would never need to know anything beyond what the family could provide. It was as if the adoption decree was supposed to do away with the child's birth family.[7]

One of the most dynamic ways you can tap into the historical and societal context present at the time of your adoption is simply to ask questions. When you bring up this issue in an attempt to understand why your parents acted as they did, some of the following questions may be helpful:

1. What was it like for you when you made the decision to adopt?
2. How did the agency or people you worked with make you feel?
3. Did you feel free to talk about the adoption with family or friends, or did you keep it quiet?
4. How did the agency advise you to discuss adoption issues with me? What did you think about the advice?

Assessing the historical context of adoption and its impact on adoptive parents is one step in preparing to communicate with them about the need to search. A second step is to take a look at the patterns of family communication that existed a generation or two ago and recognize how those patterns have changed.

Changes in Family Communication
Why didn't my adoptive parents ever ask me how I felt about adoption?

Why did I get the message that I should never question anything that had to do with my adoption or really inquire about any other issues?

Why wasn't I allowed to get angry when no one would tell me anything about my birth family?

Being raised within a family as an adopted child by the grandparents and parents of the past two generations was quite different from today. Elizabeth Fishel, in *Family Mirrors*, comments that "each new generation takes the material it has inherited, makes something new, something fitting and appropriately contemporary."[8]

Today's baby boomers who inherited relatively closed patterns of family communication from parents and grandparents have refashioned those patterns. This generation focuses much more extensively on openness, expression of feelings, and removal of masks. Looking back at what it used to be like in most families a generation ago may provide clues about why issues were left untouched, feelings untapped, and questions unanswered.

A generation ago, according to author Dolores Curran, "people paid little attention to what went on inside a family—whether there was good communication, emotional support, or trusting relationships."[9] People were only concerned about how well the family functioned.

"Our parents' generation," said Anu Sharma, "was very duty minded. Not that they weren't good at relationships, but they emphasized achievement."[10] They were concerned about how the family functioned—economically, educationally, socially, religiously. Little thought was given to how individual family members related to each other or to other issues and concerns in their life.

From the past generation to the present, the emphasis of the family is changing rapidly from considering how a family functions to how members relate to one another. The language of emotions has modified as it passes from one generation to another.[11] Fishel accounts for movement in three areas that provide explanation for the question, Why didn't we ever talk about adoption in my family?

A Broad Spectrum of Emotions

As this generation of adopted persons grapples with the issues of adoption, they do so within a wider range of acceptable emotional expression. This expression of feelings allows the presence of a dark side as well as the happy, bright side. It allows for ups as well as downs. It allows for questioning of what seems to be the norm. It is unlike the experience parents of the 1940s and 1950s encountered while growing up and passed on to their children.

Diane, an adoptee now an adoptive parent, expressed the difference between the past she encountered and the present she is attempting to create:

> In my adoptive family, no one ever brought up negative things. If we experienced a disappointment or were afraid or didn't like something, we never mentioned it. Feeling sad and talking about it just didn't happen. In my family now, my husband and I work at getting our three children to share their feelings, knowing that we probably won't like some of them. Especially now that they are nearing the teen years and adoption issues may hit them pretty hard.

More Willingness to Resolve Conflict

The "good" family of the past was taught to hide its real issues and problems. It even went further than that. The "good" family of the past had no issues and no problems.[12] Denial was a key coping mechanism. It was used to portray an image of health, wealth, and prosperity. Delores Curran explains:

> How did our ancestors cope with the problems we know they had? They coped in a way that modern parents can't and don't want to use. They wrote off the people, owning the problem as different. Over and over in my research I came upon the term *black sheep*, but this flock of sheep came in many forms. The spouse who was unfaithful or alcoholic was labeled a "ne-er do well" by the community, thus sparing the family the responsibility and shame for his or her behavior. The depressed woman was "going through her time" or "in the change," and her family was thus alleviated from blaming itself. . . . A child with learning problems was "not quite right" and those who questioned approved mores and customs were "just plain crazy."[13]

Adoptees who questioned, acted out, or otherwise rocked the boat were called ungrateful or "bad seed." Families were spared the nasty business of confronting issues by throwing it off as the fault of the adopted child.

Today's adults have taken the inheritance of denial and made something new. Today's adults show a willingness to face issues and conflict more openly, which holds true for those adults dealing with adoption issues. They do not attempt to live in denial or sweep issues under the rug. One adoptee shares her perspective:

> *I knew it would be difficult to talk to my adoptive parents about my reunion with my birth mother. The need to find her began brewing up within me months ago. I just couldn't pretend it wasn't there any longer. I will tell them what I am doing and why I am doing it. Then I will have to deal with how they respond, but that's okay.*
> —Robin Kenny, age 28

A companion to facing issues and conflicts, according to Elizabeth Fishel, is a "greater awareness about problem solving and more ingenuity in generating a whole host of solutions to puzzling family issues."[14]

More Readiness to Solve Family Problems

Years ago, a misconception existed that said "everything in good families runs smoothly and easily and something is terribly wrong if a problem arises." Today's families, according to family system theorist, Dr. Jerry Lewis, realize that problems are a part of life to be recognized and solved.[15] One adoptee's story illustrates the point:

> *When I was sixteen, I got in a lot of trouble. My parents tried to keep it quiet. They said I would outgrow it. We never talked about it; I was just told to shape up. Now that I'm nearly forty, I know those early troubles had something to do with being adopted and being terribly confused. I was just plain angry.*
>
> *Our son comes home with trouble at school pretty frequently. I don't push it off. We're working with the school and a counselor to get to the bottom of it. He joined our family by adoption at the age of three. Now at thirteen, I know things must be going on inside.*
> —Jonathan Barker, age 39

Allowing more emotional leeway, accepting feelings as they are, being willing to resolve conflict, and having a greater awareness of problem-solving techniques mark a keen difference in family communication across the generations.

How can you best tap into the patterns of communication your parents learned and handed to you? Again, by asking them key questions:

1. As you were growing up, how were issues and conflicts handled in your family?
2. What was your perception of how to handle feelings?
3. If you had a problem, how did it get resolved?
4. What would you change about the communication in your family while you were growing up?

Understanding the historical context of adoption and learning about family communication patterns of the past generation hopefully will aid you in coming to an understanding of why certain events occurred in your family the way they did. One final assessment as you talk with adoptive parents will also prove helpful.

What Do Parents Feel When a Child Says, "I'm Searching"?

"The whole question of search and reunion," according to therapist Sharon Kaplan-Roszia, "touches a whole range of feelings for adoptive parents. It reverberates clear back to the early issues of loss, grief, and self-esteem."[16] It also sends subtle messages of failure, rejection, and betrayal.

Unresolved Failure and Loss

Sandy McNeal wanted more than anything to support her daughter's need to find her birth mother. "I knew this was an important thing for her to do. I was surprised that I was initially devastated by her decision. Old memories of my inability to conceive a child came rushing back in, even twenty-three years later. Old, disturbing emotions about my own complete inadequacy surfaced—ones that I had thought were resolved years ago. I wanted to be helpful to her, but all I could say was 'go ahead if you must.' I've cried a lot about those words and wish it were different."

Inadequacy and Rejection

All that came to mind for Robert and Susan McKinney, when their son informed them of his search and impending reunion was, *Aren't we good enough for you any longer?* "We felt we had given everything we could to our son—support, love—everything. But all those feelings of doing a good job as a parent came crashing down the day he told us of his plans. We don't know why it affected us so emotionally. We know he needs to do this, but it doesn't feel good for us. We just don't feel good enough for him any longer."

Dave and Sue Van Wassenhove encouraged their daughter, Marla, to begin her search. They supported it, helped her, and even went to support group meetings with her. Still, fear accompanied them throughout the process.

"I was afraid that someone who was everything we were not would sweep Marla off her feet," Sue related. "I was afraid we would just become old hat to her and become unimportant in her life if she met her birth mother."

Dave also had fears, but of a different kind. "I have always been protective of Marla and even more so during the search. My only concern was that she was going to get hurt and, of course, I didn't want that to happen. We were prepared to go any place at any time to help her."

Three things helped Dave and Sue process their own fears. "During the search, which took two years, we saw our fears as insignificant in comparison to Marla's need," Sue commented. "We saw her hurting; we saw her identity as a person lacking. We felt compelled to help her find the truth. Marla's reassurance of her love for us and that we would always be her parents was extremely helpful. Coupled with this was our deep faith and belief that God placed our children into our hands to be their caretakers not possessors. We felt blessed, we adored her, but we also had to let her go to do what she needed to do."

Carol Demuth, an adoptee and adoption therapist, explains that although adoptive parents know the reason for their adult child's search, for some it feels like personal failure. "Some parents ask themselves a score of questions like, What does this say about our relationship? Haven't I done enough as a parent? It calls into question one's sense of competency."[17]

Incredible ambivalance is a common response to the search. "They want it for their child, but it hurts deeply," Demuth says. "On the one hand, they want their child to be healed through the reunion encounter but are pained because they were not fully adequate to provide that for them. Some parents even question if they fulfilled their nurturing role since they, in themselves, couldn't make the pain go away for their child."

Recognizing the sensitive, fragile concerns of adoptive parents is an important step in the whole process of the search and reunion. Knowing that the question may renew painful memories of loss and failure, ignite feelings of inadequacy for your adoptive parents, or fuel fears of rejection or hurt in yourself will equip you to approach your parents with sensitivity and understanding.

Dr. Severson strongly believes that an overwhelming number of adoptive parents understand.

> The essential point is that every human being on the face of the earth has a right to look into the eyes of those from whom they drew life. . . . It is my belief, heartfelt as well, that no human being would wish to deny adoptees that right once they can be helped to see the human justice of it. And certainly I do not believe that any adoptive parents whose love for the child . . . is as enduring and ennobling as any love on earth, would deny that right to his or her adopted children. But if they do not see it, it is not because they are blind; it is because their eyes have not yet opened. Love and respect and understanding are the answer, not blame and guilt.[18]

To move beyond blame, guilt, and misunderstanding is a noble goal in crossing the bridge together. To explore, understand, and to forgive your parents for lack of support or even misdirected hostility opens doors to keeping the relationship open and healthy.

In the effort to meet these goals, you may smooth out the pathway ahead by asking the following questions:

1. How painful was it for you to realize you would never have a child by birth? (if applicable)
2. Who helped you deal with that loss? Anyone?

3. What kind of feelings do you remember experiencing as I became part of the family?
4. Have you had feelings of being a failure or inadequate as it relates to our relationship?
5. What are your greatest fears about my searching?
6. What can I do so that we can share this experience together?

As young or middle-aged adopted persons step from behind the veil of secrecy to open doors and windows that were previously locked, they do so at what feels like great risk to their relationship with their adoptive parents and eventually to their relationship with birth family members. Those who have walked through it can speak from their experiences with insight on what to expect from adoptive parents.

NAVIGATING THREATENING WATERS

Unfortunately, I can tell people how not to deal with their adoptive parents. I always told my parents I would search, but when I began, I hid it all from them. When my birth mother was found on the East coast and we made arrangements to see her, I made up lies as to where we were going and what we were doing. It wasn't until my lies got too big that I finally told them the truth. They were not hurt that I was searching. They were desperately hurt about the lies. The subject is rarely brought up now. I hope someday they will feel that our relationship again will be open, trusting, and honest.
—Majorie Jefferson, age 31

My adoptive parents have encouraged me to try to find my birth parents for my own peace of mind and for medical information. I honestly don't believe my mom means it. I think she's worried that I will forget who raised and loved me over the years. My dad is open about how he feels. He doesn't want to know anything. He said it would hurt too much. As far as not sharing this with adoptive parents, I think one should share, no matter how they feel. If they aren't told about the search, and they find out, it could hurt them even more. In this case, honesty is the best policy.
—Darlene Washington, age 33

I told my mom about the search for my birth parents and let my mom tell my dad. He wasn't thrilled when I began my search and our relationship was strained for years because we were on different sides of this issue. It

was a very hard subject to discuss and still is. When I'm happy and want to share my happy news, naturally the first people I want to tell are my parents so they can share in my happiness. But my dad doesn't share in my happiness and I'm sad he feels hurt. I know that deep down my father was and still is afraid his daughter would be hurt and rejected. I think my parents were both afraid of losing me. I make sure that I show in my actions and words that my relationship with them hasn't changed. The only thing that will prove my love hasn't changed is time.
—Mary Meaker, age 28

I think my dad has difficulty with the reunion because he really believed that the only family I have is my adoptive family. He doesn't seem to understand the loss I've felt all my life. I think he is insecure about the reunion because deep down he fears I may choose my birth family over my adoptive family. I think he blames himself for my search—if he and Mom had done a better job I wouldn't need to search. It's as if his love should have been enough for me to forget the fact that I was someone else's daughter first. What I've done to deal with this is to visit them more frequently. I want to reinforce the fact that my reunion with my birth parents did not change anything.
—Allison McGaffy, 29

During my search, I shared all the information with them as the process took place. They saw my excitement. However, the relationship I have with them didn't change. I still called them as often and visited them the same amount. I tried not to focus constantly on my search. Now I don't focus on time spent with my other mother when I am with them.
—Martha Schilling, age 42

One thing I wanted to do was honor my adoptive mother during the reunion period of my search. On the day I was to meet my birth mother for the very first time, I sent flowers to my adoptive mother, assuring her of my deep love for her and deep commitment to my adoptive family.
—Andrew West, age 29

From a letter to adoptive parents following a reunion:

My dear Mom and Dad,
    I hope that someday, somehow, you will understand my love for you. I never wanted to hurt you by searching for my birth family. I hope I

have not done so. No matter how close I become to my birth parents, or how I accept them as "my other family," I do hope you know how important you are to me. I am "your child," but I am also the child of Daniel and MaryAnn. Each of you has given me such tremendous gifts—all of which I could never repay. Daniel and MaryAnn gave me life, and you taught me how to live it and loved me no matter what. I could never repay the debt I owe to either of you. The best I can hope for at this time is that you will accept my relationship with my birth family and know that my love for you does not diminish because of my love for them.

    Lovingly, Rebecca, age 24

Contrary to what some people think about why adoptees search, I was able to search because my adoptive parents did such a great job rearing me to mature, well-adjusted adulthood. The foundation they laid made me secure enough to take this risk.

—Betsie Norris, age 34

SECTION·TWO

Starting the Journey Back

---✣---

CHAPTER FOUR

PREPARING EMOTIONALLY FOR THE SEARCH

❖

Once I made the decision to search,

there came a great sense of relief.

I had thought about it for years,

but when I made a decision,

there came a sense of peace.

BETSIE NORRIS

Judy hurriedly finished the letter she wanted to mail. She was writing the agency that placed her in her adoptive home. For months Judy struggled over the decision to search and also with discussing it with her adoptive parents. A weekend visit home convinced her it was the right thing to do and the right time to do it. Today, she began. The struggle of "should I or shouldn't I" was over. A deep sense of relief followed her throughout the day, even though she knew there would be bumps in the road ahead.

Making the decision to initiate the search is a critical turning point in the life of an adopted person. As he walks a path that may link unknown events and people from an unknown past to the events and people of the present, preparation is an absolute necessity, and he must face a multitude of concerns.

First, the searcher will encounter unexpected emotions that may propel him into confusion, anger, fear, even depression at a depth which he has not yet experienced. Second, he must learn to recognize unrealistic expectations within himself and balance those with probable reality. Third, he should be aware of the people he will meet and their reactions, both positive and negative. A searcher must have a reasonable perception of what circumstances he may find regarding his birth family. Finally, the searcher must know how and where to gain support, for this is a journey not to be undertaken alone.

HANDLING THE EMOTIONAL ROLLER COASTER

The only thing for certain when plowing new ground is that unknown ruts, rocks, even boulders can block progress. As the adopted person plows new ground in his search, he may find himself profoundly confused at the depth and breadth of his emotions.

I Didn't Know I Would Feel So Angry

Every day I rushed out to the mailbox to see if the agency sent any information. It finally came and I was completely thrown off by my reaction.

What my adoptive parents told me didn't match what the agency sent. Nothing matched! I thought my birth parents were young and unmarried. I could live with that. But as it turned out, they were married with other children. My birth father was an alcoholic and abandoned my mother. She just couldn't handle another child.

After I read that, I felt such rage at everyone—my adoptive parents, the agency, and especially my birth father for being such a loser. I had never felt anything so deeply.

—Jonathan, age 32

The search process can trigger a great deal of buried anger. Blocked from expressing unwelcome feelings about the adoption as a younger person, the adoptee's emotions often vault to the surface as incredible rage.

Betsie Norris, in her work as president of Adoption Network Cleveland, a large support and advocacy group in Ohio, often sees that anger and believes it originates from and is directed toward many different people.

At whom or what is the anger directed? The anger may be aimed at:

+ The birth mother—Why couldn't you keep me?
+ The birth father—Why couldn't you support your family? Why couldn't you get your life together?
+ The agency—Why couldn't you help my mother, or why didn't you share the truth?
+ The adoptive parents—Why didn't you talk to me more about my adoption; why didn't you tell me the truth?

Whatever the source, legitimate or misdirected anger is something many adoptees face. What to do with it then becomes the issue.

While often viewed as something to avoid, anger can become the ally of the adoptee. Betty Jean Lifton comments,

> We must remember that no matter how painful these waves of grief and anger are, they are part of the ongoing process of mourning that comes with reclaiming one's lost emotions and integrating them into the self. Adoptees find it hard to believe at the time, but the chaos carries healing in its wake.[1]

An adopted person's anger en route to healing is best encountered with help. Adoption counselor, Barbara Wentz, strongly suggests the adopted person seek an open ear from a third party as anger surfaces. "Someone outside the relationship who would not be affected by the venting of the adoptee's anger can best be that buffer. It could be a therapist or a trusted friend who understood the dynamics of the healing process."[2]

Anger is one emotion that catches the adopted person off guard. Sadness and depression are two more.

Why Do I Feel So Blue?

Before I made the first call to my birth mother, I was excited, energized by the upcoming reunion. After that first call, I felt overwhelmed with sadness . . . even depression. In fact, through the evening and into the

next day, I could only sit and cry. For days afterward, I felt as if a balloon had burst. I kept asking myself, Why am I reacting like this? It was a great contact. I should be happy!
—Christine Walton, age 27

Some adoptees, according to Betsie Norris, may for the first time be dealing with the losses adoption created in their lives. For some, the sound of their birth mother's voice is enough to invoke the incredible sadness they kept buried within.

"When an adoptee finds a birth parent," says Dr. Joyce Maguire Pavao, "he is often not prepared for the depression that comes with that. The better the reunion, the harder it is sometimes.

"One reason," she continued, "is that there is a lost history. You meet the person twenty years later and you realize you missed all of his history, all of his connections. There is a real sadness about that loss."[3]

What Am I Afraid Of?

As an adopted person steps onto the rickety bridge connecting the unknown past to the unknown future, she places herself at great peril. The perceived reality of that peril grows as the adoptee confronts the taboos connected to the desire to search. The peril broadens as the adopted person faces the risk of losing relationships—first, her adoptive parents and then, perhaps, her birth family. The peril feels overwhelming as the adopted person attempts to scale the seemingly insurmountable wall of the adoption system. A sense of peril creates fear.

Fear can be an immobilizing emotion. It can temporarily block or permanently stop an adopted person's attempts to locate birth family members. What do some adoptees say they fear?

Rejection . . . Again

I was afraid of being rejected again by someone I loved. Even though I'd never met my father and didn't know him, I loved him anyway! How could I not love the one person on earth whom others told me I was so much like. I was afraid that once I finally found the one person whose biological blueprint formed my life . . . he would say "nope, you're not like me and I'm not interested in knowing you!"
—Susan Friel-Williams, age 40

I put off beginning my search for over ten years. The thing I feared the most was that my birth mother would have nothing to do with me. My

worst fear did come true at the beginning. She denied knowing anything about me. Then she said she didn't want to see me. My friends supported me through this and encouraged me to give her time. At age seventy-six, it probably really disrupted her life. About four months after the initial contacts, I received a note that opened a window to our new, yet very fragile, relationship.
—Sally Allen, age 45

Stirring Up Painful Memories

I had to overcome the fear that I would make my birth mother remember things she didn't want to remember. Maybe the circumstances of my birth were horribly painful for her and she had buried them long ago. If I came into her life, I wondered what might happen inside of her.
—MaryAnn Batty, age 33

Ruining a Parent's Life

It took a lot of courage for me to pick up the phone and call my birth mother. Regardless of our blood tie, she was a total stranger to me and I to her. I was afraid she would hang up or deny that she was my birth mother. I was afraid I would "ruin her life" by contacting her. So many people told me she had moved on with her life and wouldn't want this interruption. I was afraid they were right. But I called. And she didn't hang up or deny she was my birth mother. I didn't ruin her life; even though she had moved on, she had never forgotten me.
—Dana Kressierer, age 24

Displeasing a Parent

I had a real fear that my birth mother would be disappointed in the type of person I had turned out to be. What if I was a total disappointment to her? What if the life choices I had made were not the correct choices in her eyes? I had to convince myself I wasn't a "bad" person before I took the plunge and decided to search for her. I kept telling myself over and over that I was a "good" person. The reason I had to tell myself that was because I had serious doubts that this person I was searching for would agree with me. It's amazing how much control my birth mother had over my thoughts, feelings, and emotions about myself when I had absolutely no idea who she was.
—Mary Meeker, 28

Losing Control

I had a fear of losing control of my life. I felt that once I got the call, I could no longer control the search. When you choose to search you have all the control. You have the option to stop and start before going on to the next step. The match happened so fast—within a week and a half of registering with ISRR (International Soundex Reunion Registry, P.O. Box 2312, Carson City, NV 89702; 702-882-7755). I never prepared myself for getting the call. I never had the opportunity to even consider slowing down or stopping. Some people in my search group got information and they could back out and prepare for what might happen. I had to quickly prepare to meet people whom I had never known.
—Beverly Perry, age 34

Still Feeling Different

When I became a teenager, I went through a period where I felt so different from everyone else in my adoptive home. I didn't look like anyone. I made a promise to myself that when I was old enough, I would try to find my birth family. I know it sounds ridiculous, but after all of those years of needing to look like someone, I was afraid I wouldn't look like them either.
—Jody Young, age 28

Finding Deadends or Death

I was desperately afraid toward the end of my search that if I didn't find my father that something would happen to him and I'd never get the chance to actually "know" him and find out what he's like. I guess this fear was the biggest factor in my decision to start my search again at age thirty-five. I knew his age . . . and I knew of his early lifestyle. It was imperative I find him while he was still living.
—Susan Friel-Williams, age 40

Feeling sadness, facing rejection, disappointment, painful memories, loss of control, and deadends—all are legitimate experiences encountered by adopted persons as they prepare to cross over the bridge leading to reunion. Facing emotional upheavals prior to and during the early days of the reunion and confronting sadness and fear will build strength into the emotional backbone of the adult adoptee. Two other emotions may catch many searchers off guard.

Overwhelmed and Overloaded

Kathy's reunion with her birth family went well. It continued to go well for about two months and then the relationship became strained and tense. A

60

major reason for the disruption of a budding relationship was that Kathy felt overwhelmed emotionally by the response from her birth family. She lost her space, did not know how to regain it gracefully, and felt guilty for feeling as she did.

Kathy had been searching for her birth mother for over eight months when her mother was finally located just one hour away. Within a few hours of the first phone call, Kathy was sitting in her living room surrounded by many "new" relatives. The reunion had all the signs of being one of those storybook endings. However, after the first contact, both mother and daughter rushed to build a relationship, ignoring advice to take it slow. They talked with each other daily on the phone, and Kathy's birth mother became possessive of Kathy's time as she attempted to make up for lost years. She expected Kathy to feel just like family and take part in other extended family gatherings. Kathy, overwhelmed by her birth mother's attention and expectations, was confused by her feelings and at a loss as to what to do.

Adoption counselor, Barbara Wentz, in her work with all members of the adoption triad during the search process, sees this as a common problem.

"I compare the meeting of the birth parents and their child to that of young people who meet and fall in love. It's like being on a high where you can never get enough of being with someone." Acting on these feelings can do much damage to the fragile relationship unless there is proper emotional preparation, warns Wentz.

"I recommend that there is no face-to-face contact without laying some groundwork. That groundwork can be in the form of letters and/or phone calls. Figuring out one's boundaries prior to meeting will help keep emotionally charged plans from overwhelming either party."

All during the search and reunion process, in order to keep your emotional life in balance, Wentz recommends the following:

- Keep the other components of your life stable—don't make other major life changes.
- Maintain and keep other healthy relationships—avoid becoming obsessed with the newfound person.
- Keep a journal of events and feelings so you can evaluate your progress.

Akin to feeling overwhelmed by the emotional attention generated by the reunion is feeling overloaded.

Author Michele McColm writes:

Because adoptees have lived for so many years with little or no information about their birth family, their curiosity and their need drives them to collect so much information so quickly. . . . Wanting to meet increasing numbers of birth family members, even though the original and ultimate goal was to meet her birth mother is evidence of the depth of the adoptee's primal need to solidify her identity. . . . All this activity leads to depression and/or exhaustion.[4]

In one day, Randy had met his birth parents, both sets of grandparents, three birth siblings and numberless nieces and nephews. He had listened to countless stories about the birth family. When he got home that night, he could barely relate the experiences of the day to his wife. All he wanted was to be alone. That feeling continued for days.

Betty Jean Lifton encountered these same experiences during the early days of her reunion with her birth mother. She writes:

The decision for time out is not always a conscious one. In Lost and Found I wrote about the emotional turmoil many adoptees, including myself felt. . . . I was so overwhelmed with anxiety and guilt after meeting my mother that I fell through the trap door of self, down to what felt like rock bottom. . . . For the next two months I withdrew from everything around me, staying still until I could regain the . . . energy to climb back up into the outside world again.[5]

Riding out the emotional roller coaster brought on by the search and reunion may bring a new level of self-awareness and understanding. Although frightening and intense, the ride is a necessary part of preparing for the reunion and of the healing process. There's another crucial preparation step.

Examine Expectations About the New "Family"

Deep longings create profound expectations. Postponed desires inflate one's expectations of the outcome. For the adopted person whose inmost yearning is to reconnect to birth family members, examining one's hope for the reunion experience may prevent unnecessary disappointment or heartbreak.

An important step in preparing emotionally for the search is to understand what expectations other adopted persons have experienced. Betty Jean Lifton addresses three types of expectations adoptees often encounter.

"Many adoptees have expectations going into the reunion that cannot be met," says Lifton. "The adoptee expects to be immediately transformed and not to be the same person, but the wonderful idealized self they might have been if they had not been adopted. They wake up the morning after the reunion and find they are still the same."

Continuing, she said, "Some adoptees expect to be instantly healed. Like Pinocchio. He is just a piece of wood and suddenly he comes to life with all the emotions. The adoptee identifies with Pinocchio and will say 'I felt dead before,' but now I feel. The problem is, if you have never felt before, you have never really known what grief or anger is or what loss is. If you allow yourself to feel for the first time, you can be overwhelmed by the feelings."

A third expectation not always met is a surprise to many adopted persons. Lifton says, "The adoptee is shocked to find he may not have unconditional love from his birth mother. They think all other people not separated from their mothers are getting unconditional love and they should be getting that too at the reunion."[6] What they find in some cases is that the birth mother does not have the emotional strength to enter the relationship or she has constructed a life and family exclusive of the possibility that the birth child may someday want to reenter her life. She may not be emotionally available to the adoptee, Lifton adds, or she might be mentally unstable or even dead.

Anticipating transformation, healing, or unconditional love are what many adoptees have hoped for as they enter the reunion with birth family members. What are some ways to deal with one's expectations?

Realize That Expectations Change

My expectations changed constantly—both during my search and after my reunion. I expected my birth parents and me to become very good friends; at other times I expected them to suddenly not want anything more to do with me. The expectations of rejection were most pronounced when I told them things about myself of which I was ashamed. I wanted my birth parents to be proud of me and thought they would reject me if they learned of my mistakes and regrets. I was finally able to overcome this when I realized they too had made mistakes and I still accepted them, flaws and all. As friends, none of us will ever have to be perfect.
—Dana Kressierer, age 25

I Tried Not to Have Expectations

I tried not to expect anything from the reunion. My philosophy is that without expectations there can't be disappointments and anything that does happen is acceptable. Of course, I couldn't help fantasizing I would

find my birth mother and we would get along wonderfully and live happily ever after.
—Carol Wallenfelsz, age 23

I Tried to Have Low Expectations

I never had high expectations during my search. I always told myself that if somehow I could just have a photograph of my birth mother, that would be enough. Or if I could stand across the street from her and someone would say, "That is your birth mother," seeing her without her knowing it, I wouldn't ask for anything else. So I really don't think I had high expectations about how things would or should be.
—Shelly McKinney, age 32

I Tried to Keep My Expectations in Perspective

I tried to look at every aspect of my search from the perspective of each person currently involved or those who would be involved in the future. What were their feelings and fears? How would this affect their lives as well as those close to them? I read a lot of literature and studied different aspects of searching from those who had found or were still involved in the searching process. This helped me keep things in perspective.
—Michelle Buchanan, age 27

I Tried to Look at Both Sides of the Coin

The possibility of a reunion was too important to me to let myself get carried away with the fantasy of a perfect reunion. I just kept my mind open and tried to keep my heart out of it. I knew that if I searched and found my birth mother and things turned out badly, I would still be satisfied knowing whatever it was I learned. If I learned that my birth mother wanted nothing to do with me, okay, at least I knew. I needed some idea of what she was feeling. I taught myself to be open to anything and to accept anything.
—Carol Wallenfelz, age 23

Processing emotional issues and balancing expectations are important preliminary steps in the search process. Understanding who you may meet along the way and what circumstances may confront you are also important steps in the early months of the search and reunion.

Those You Meet Along the Way

From finding birth information to meeting the birth parent—all is a fragile process for many adult adoptees. As you search, you will encounter many people along the way—some who will join in the moment, others who will dampen your enthusiasm. Who are these people?

The Agency Social Worker

As the dynamics of the adoption search are understood by more and more in the adoption field, hopefully adoptees will deal with a more receptive audience when calling for search information. However, the search will still be controlled by the social worker's own interpretation of what is considered "non-identifying" information. That intepretation dictates what and how much information they are open to sharing. One adoptee didn't let a negative experience dampen her dream of finding her birth family.

> *The agency acted as if I had no business looking for myself. They were paternalistic and really bad for my self-esteem. They felt they had no obligation to me because I was never their client. They felt their order of priorities were the birth mother and my adoptive parents. I felt like a nonentity to them. One worker interpreted my need to search as being unhappy with their original arrangement. If I had it to do over again, I would not employ the agency to handle my search and I would have been braver in making the first contact myself.*
> —Nancy Walker, age 30

Federal and State Office Personnel

Information crucial to putting the adoptee's life puzzle together is filed away in federal, state, and county document offices. One of the most frustrating experiences for many has been to hit the wall when attempting to get information. Some withholding is required by law and out of the hands of the clerk. Other information is legally obtainable by the adopted person and is withheld at the discretion of the employee. Mary Jo Rillera suggests that in dealing with these offices and the blockage of legimate information, you should proceed through channels to a high supervisory level. "If they are within the law, you must just hope they are humane and caring people."[7] One young woman found a positive and helpful person at a large county office.

> *As I searched through records in a large metropolitan county courthouse, a clerk volunteered to help.*
> *"This is highly unusual," she informed me. "Just two weeks ago a man was in here looking for the same information. Over two months ago a young woman asked me these same questions. I gave them this address."*

Out of the multitude of personnel at the courthouse, this clerk helped all three of us. That afternoon, I learned I had a sister and a brother and had a way to make contact.[8]
—Randy Hopkins, age 38

Friends and Acquaintances

The people an adoptee often seeks support from are friends outside the family circle. They are people with whom real feelings, fears, and concerns can be openly shared. It's important to select carefully with whom you share the dream of reunion . . . for you may meet with encouragement or cold water. Jan Campbell, who found out about her adoption at age forty-four and then wanted to search, received a variety of reactions.

The reactions I got from friends fell into two categories: supportive and suspicious. Supportive friends ask now and then if I've heard anything from Peggy (my birth mother). The "suspicious" reactions came from "parent" type people . . . especially other adoptive parents. They report to me that their children have no interest in digging into the past and the implication is that I shouldn't either. Let well enough alone.

People Who Exploit

When Mark Holland finally found the search group in his local community, he had already spent nearly $2,000. He had hired what he believed to be an honest private investigator. However, it seemed that with each passing day the investigator required more and more money and Mark didn't see much result.

Betsie Norris advises that adoptees explore all the alternatives. "Many can search for themselves with the help of search/support groups located all over the country. Some people may choose to pay an investigator because they may not have enough time or energy to do the search themselves, but the process of the search is lost when an individual is not actively involved. I strongly encourage searching adoptees to be as involved as possible and definitely to join a support group."

Betsie adds, "When hiring someone else to do the search, the searching person should ask a lot of questions about what the investigator's procedures are and how much the payment will be. Don't give payment up front. The searching individual should make sure the information comes back to him and that he maintains control of the pace of the search as well as how contact will be made. Everything should be clear up front."

Responding to people who come along the path in the midst of your journey requires you to react with tact and wisdom. Learning about what circumstances you may find regarding the history of your birth family and your birth requires those same skills.

What You May Find
At the age of twelve, Robert Anderson found out that he was adopted. As he began to explore his background, he discovered a painful secret. He had been sold to his adoptive parents for a substantial amount of money. The doctor had falsified the original birth certicate leaving him no clues as to his birth parents' identity. Robert was a black market baby. The door to his past was forever sealed. Circumstances for other adoptees have been just as traumatic.

Finding the Records Destroyed
In the late 1950s, a maternity home in a midwestern state placed hundreds of babies into adoptive homes. Susan McGowen, now in her late thirties, was one of those infants. However, when she began her search, she was devastated to find that the founder of the home had died and her family, seeing no need "for all the clutter," destroyed the records from the maternity home. She could not talk to her adoptive parents about her need to find information and now she felt she had no way of finding out anything.

Finding a Criminal History
Once Richard Henry discovered his birth family name, the search process went relatively quickly. His birth father had left a lasting impression upon the neighboring community. Richard's father was easily located, for he had been incarcerated for years. Richard felt shame and embarrassment over what he had found. Eventually, knowing the truth helped Richard put his entire life into a context he would not have had otherwise.

Finding Abandonment
Tracy Shepherd could hardly believe what her parents told her regarding her adoption. For years she had been told her birth parents died in a car accident. Finally they told her the truth. Tracy had been left on a park bench late one evening and discovered by a passing patrolman. No clues to her birth parents were ever found. She had not only been abandoned physically at birth, she was abandoned emotionally, historically, forever.

Finding Death
For Tina Ricketts, the issue of the search had consumed her every waking moment for the last several months. Recently she learned that her birth

parents were dead . . . an option she had not allowed herself to consider. Finding that her parents were gone was a sad discovery, but Tina was able to find conclusion to her search through contacts with other family members.

Finding difficult birth family circumstances presents adoptees with a dilemma—what to do with what they know. For many, although the information is unpleasant or inconclusive, it provides them with a sense of completion, a sense of connectedness to the past.

Juggling the emotions, facing the fears, weighing the overload, confronting people and issues—what a task for one person to handle! How can you best prepare emotionally for the search? Those who have done so tell us how.

GOOD ADVICE

Although I'm an advocate for feeling emotions strongly and deeply, I advise keeping expectations in perspective. Do not allow fantasies to cloud reality. I would change nothing and do nothing differently than I did. I tried to allow things just to happen. I was fortunate—our reunion could not have happened any more beautifully than it did.
—Carol Wallenfelsz, age 23

Never give up searching, but have a strong faith in God and in yourself to accept whatever you find. Then go on with life. Make sure you have a good network of support to guide you and help you make wise decisions.
—Tammy Pasela, age 35

The first thing I try to get across to those I help in searches is that unless they are comfortable with their own feelings and willing to accept the bad as well as the good, they are probably not ready to search. The one thing that tips me they are ready is their concern for not making waves in their birth parents' lives.

I also tell them, don't give up. Sometimes you need to step back and go at the search from a different angle . . . but just don't stop. Take a vacation. Go to the beach or mountains. Come back renewed and start again. You are healing while you seek those lost loved ones and the missing pieces of your own story.
—Susan Friel-Williams, age 40

I would advise others involved in the search process to keep a positive attitude in dealing with their expectations. Often searches take a long time

and are taxing on the emotions. Get involved in a good support group. Look at your search from every angle . . . see how if affects you as well as others who will sooner or later become involved. But the main thing is to keep a positive attitude . . . one day you will find what you seek.
—Shelly McKinney, age 32

Finding your birth parents will not solve any of your problems; in fact, it will probably create more problems. But it will help you understand yourself better and it will give you new strength to face your problems head-on and overcome them. If you feel, as I did, the need to search is so great that it just can't be overcome, then do it. Search for yourself, and realize that no matter what the outcome, you have completed an amazing task and you should be proud of yourself.
—Dana Kressierer, age 25

Our society has supported a huge amount of denial regarding some of the realities of adoption. In my search I had to acknowlege there had indeed been a loss. Before joining a support group of adoptees and birth parents, everyone I knew had only emphasized what I gained from adoption. I felt alone in realizing there was a lot more to it than that. What a relief when I found others who were speaking honestly and openly about the realities I knew but had never dared put into words.

As my search progressed, I openly talked with my friends and family about what I was doing. Many were very supportive. However, it was only the other searching adoptees whom I felt truly understood what was driving me to search.

It was a very emotional time for me with many ups and downs. I can't imagine having gone through it without a supportive community behind me.

Since my reunion, involvement in an adoption group has remained an important part of my life for several reasons. Along with my own personal benefit, I feel committed to helping the system change to meet triad members' needs better and to being there for others so they don't have to go through this alone.
—Betsie Norris, age 34

CHAPTER FIVE

INITIATING THE SEARCH AND FIRST CONTACT

❖

In a drawer, in a bedroom in Milwaukee,

there is a photograph of a baby and her

mother. The camera lens does not extend

to the mother's face, just her arms holding

the baby to her chest. The baby is dressed

in a white gown. A hood pulled down

over her head reveals a tuft of red hair.

A peculiar silence surrounds this picture,

a silence that has gone on for twenty-five

years. For reasons unknown to them,

on this day they begin to open up to each

other and speak of the baby they gave up

those many years ago.[1]

ABOUT BETSIE'S BIRTH PARENTS

The red-haired little girl always knew she was adopted. From her earliest memories her parents had told her how much they had wanted a child and that she was special to them. They told her of the love her birth parents shared for each other and of their lack of readiness to care for a child. They loved each other, they loved her; but they had to let her go.

Once, when she was very young, the red-haired little girl and her adoptive mother went downtown to a building in an older part of the city where they lived. The mother told her inquisitive daughter this was the adoption agency. As they walked slowly down the dim hallway, the mother pointed to a room and said to her wondering child, "This is where you came from."

Even at such a young age, the little girl felt odd about that. It was a strange feeling to think the beginning of her life could only be traced to a stone building that seemed like a cold, unfriendly kind of place.

That first trip to see the building fed the little girl's curiosity. On many trips downtown her mother would point to the building and say something about it. She wanted her little girl to know all about her adoption story.

High school graduation brought a new adventure to the red-haired adolescent as she moved out of her parents' home into her own apartment. Work and college loomed ahead of her. However, with this step into adulthood and departure from her adoptive home, she began to think more about two other people. She began to think a lot about the other mother and father. *What did she look like? Does she have red hair? Where is she now? What about her young love? Who was he and where was he? Did he just walk away from her?*

More than once she pulled the heavy, awkward city directory out of the drawer. She was going to find the agency that handled her adoption. Anxiety gripped her. Questions flooded her. What if they won't answer my questions? What if they think it strange? Am I being disloyal to my parents? Does anyone else ever wonder? And the most threatening—do I have a right to know? She didn't dial the number. She couldn't, not yet.

One afternoon while walking through a college bookstore, a book called *The Adoption Triangle* caught her eye. Pulling it off the shelf, she realized she had made an important find, *a miraculous find*, one that would change the course of her life as well as those of her adoptive parents and birth parents.

That fall evening she stayed up throughout the night absorbing the contents of the book. She discovered she wasn't alone, for others had asked the unaskable questions. She learned that she wasn't disloyal to her adoptive parents, that she could love them deeply and still have a need to find her roots. She also uncovered a spectacular secret—it was all right for her to know.

The miraculous find paved the way to begin searching for her birth family. It told her how to find support and how to look. It told her to contact the adoption agency and encouraged her to contact a national support group, which she did immediately. From that group contact, she learned something of incredible importance. She learned that she could have the key that would open the door to her mystery—her birth certificate. She wrote for it at once.

Not long after that, a manila envelope arrived at her home. Carefully opening it she pulled out a copy of something. It was her birth certificate. She saw a name—Victoria Faith Boyer. At first she thought it was her mother's name. After studying it further, she realized it was her very own name. *I'm Betsie,* she thought to herself, *but I'm also Victoria Faith.* For her, "it was like discovering a secret passageway in a house you had lived in for years."[2] She had another name, another identity, one that had been handed to her by a woman she had yet to know.

The birth certificate told her of a place not so very far away, Wallingford, Pennsylvania, and of a street where her birth mother had lived. It told her that her mother was twenty-one, not the teenager she had envisioned all her life. She knew she had to go to Wallingford, but first she had to get the information from the adoption agency. It was the right time now. She called them.

When the agency returned her call, they told her they had her information and would mail it to her. She told them she would be right down to get it, not wishing to wait a few more days. The clerk couldn't understand her hurry, but she didn't care.

The material in hand, she anxiously read it. "Your birth mother was sixteen years old and blonde. She had moved to the area to conceal the pregnancy. Your birth father was seventeen and also blond."

The young woman didn't know what to believe. The ages confused her. However, she knew enough about genetics to know—her red hair told her—this paper from the adoption agency was wrong. The birth certificate, of course, had to be right. She would follow that lead. It led her to that city hundreds of miles away.

The search became somewhat of an obsession. She made many trips to Wallingford hoping to find anything that would connect her to her birth mother. One particular trip she went to the high school where her birth mother had graduated. Nervous, yet determined, she braved the potential questions of a high school librarian and asked to see the yearbook for 1956.

Within moments she looked at the face of the young woman who had loved her, kissed her, and said goodbye. No words could describe the feeling.

With much information in hand from her birth mother's class reunion list, the young woman returned to her own city reenergized. She had found who her mother had married and where she was now living. She decided to make contact. The young woman was within moments of connecting with the woman who had given her life.

Preparing to make the most important call of her life was intensely emotional. The young woman composed a script she was determined to follow. She had to be prepared to be rejected, but she just couldn't be rejected! Part of her birth name had been Faith. She felt it was a message to her. Besides, how could someone who named her Victoria Faith reject her?

She picked up the phone and dialed the number. Three short rings and a woman answered the phone.

"Is this Edith?" she asked. "My name is Betsie Norris and I'm calling you from Cleveland, Ohio. I have something very important to talk to you about. Is this a good time? This is a very important and private matter."

Continuing, she told her mother, " I was born in Cleveland on February 20, 1960 and put up for adoption. I am happy and very well adjusted. I don't want to hurt you or your family or disrupt your life, but I'd like to talk with you. My research about my background has led me to you. I know this is quite a shock. Do you need some time?"

Before Betsie even finished, the woman on the other end flooded her with questions. "Where do you live? Do you have red hair? What do you do for a living? A nurse? Your grandmother had red hair and was a nurse."

She enthusiastically continued, "I have been praying for this call for twenty-six years . . . Bob will be thrilled."

"Who is Bob?" the young woman asked.

"Your father, my husband."

Had she heard right? He hadn't turned his back. He was there all the time!

"We'll call you tonight," the older woman said. "What is your number? Can I have your address?"

My address, Betsie thought sadly. *My mother doesn't know my address.*

"Just a minute, before you go, what time was I born?" the child asked her mother.

"In the evening," came the reply. "Right at dinner time—6:01."

The red-haired woman hung up the phone, overwhelmed to learn that her life would now embrace the lives of two families. She now had five brothers—three on one side, her birth family; two on the other. She felt very rich.[3]

Walking through the journey of the search and reunion with Betsie Norris and her family touches a deep, emotional chord. Her story paints a vivid picture of what experiences may lie ahead for adopted persons. In Betsie's case, the search, which took six months, encountered some brick walls of wrong information, delays, and blanks. But persistence paid off.

For every searcher, whether young adult or approaching mid-life or beyond, following some basic guidelines will help put the scattered pieces of the puzzle together.

Recognize the Emotional Stages of the Search

One: "This Isn't a Big Deal"—Neutrality

"No big deal," Michael said—at least at first. At twenty-six, he decided it would be interesting to know something about his background. He simply wrote the adoption agency for medical and background information.

In this first stage, according to author Jayne Askin, "the searcher is commonly somewhat removed from the emotions of searching." Like Michael, the adoptee often "expresses the reason for starting the search in very neutral terms and concentrates on the mechanics of the search, feeling no strong commitment to it."[4]

Two: "What—No Information?"—Anger and Frustration

As bits of information come to the adoptee, the neutral attitude is replaced with emotions brought on by encountering reality. What Michael had not counted upon was that suppressed feelings and needs about his adoptive status would surface with incredible intensity as small amounts of information emerged and other crucial pieces were not available.

As the searcher attempts to gather information and confronts roadblocks, incredible frustration and anger can surface. For the first time in the search, he may realize that important information about himself is not readily his simply by birthright.

Askin believes anger is a critical step in working through the stages of the search. However, she cautions the searcher not to get stuck in this stage to the degree it prevents him from processing deeper feelings. "Rage may cover feelings of rejection, insecurity, and guilt that have started to surface, or may sharpen them in instances where the searcher was already aware of his feelings," Askin said.[5]

Three: "It Consumes All My Thoughts and My Time" — Obsession

Once a searcher finds himself in the midst of the search, he is often surprised at the burning persistence of his obsession. Michael found himself thinking about the search when he woke up and he stayed preoccupied with it while attempting to get work done at the office. He vacillated between anger and resentment at being blocked from information and anxiousness and doubt that he would ever find his birth parents.

"Becoming obsessed with the search is normal," commented Betsie Norris. "It's all part of the process. When it happens, the adoptee might feel as though he's losing his mind or emotional control. He may find himself talking about the search all the time to anyone who will listen," she added.

Another adoptee, Dana Kressierer, at twenty-five felt the same obsession.

> I was very surprised at how much my search mattered to me. I really became obsessed about finding my birth parents, and every new piece of information I received just made me more determined to someday find them.

Four: "This is Overwhelming" — Withdrawal

Many searchers find themselves overwhelmed with frustrations, disappointments, anxieties, and setbacks. Sometimes, for a period of time, they must withdraw from the fray. Dana Kressierer experienced this stage of withdrawal.

> Searching often seems like a never-ending process; there's always one more letter to write, one more phone call to make, and one more brick wall to run into. I often felt overwhelmed, and I doubted sometimes if my search was worth all the time, money, and frustration that went along with the process. When this happened, I tried to step back for a few days and clear my head. I would talk with other searchers about my progress or lack thereof, and try to get suggestions from them.

Some searchers, according to Betsie, may step back from the process for more than just a few days. Some step back for months, even years. What happens is that the search brings up feelings they were unaware of and need time to process.

Five: "Whatever Happens Is Okay"—Acceptance

Michael, after spending months in the search mode and finding one brick wall after another, made a decision not to carry his effort any further for a while. He was at peace with this decision. Jayne Askin calls this stage acceptance. This stage comes as the adoptee accepts *whatever* is discovered. This can mean he may decide to continue the search or not. Either way, he accepts it. It could also mean that the searcher, having found valuable information, decides to take the opportunity to open the door to the new relationship.[6]

Recognizing your own personal stage of the search is important. Another essential guideline is to understand your personal rights.

LEARN ABOUT THE ADOPTION LAWS WITHIN YOUR OWN STATE

Every state governs its own adoption law regarding birth and adoption records. Procedures and what information is obtainable to the adoptee widely vary. Here are examples of four state laws:

From the state of Alabama: Code of Alabama, Section 38-7-13.

> Any person who has arrived at the age of 19 and who was placed by the department or by a licensed child-placing agency shall have the right to receive from the department or child-placing agency information concerning his placement; except, that the name and address of a natural parent or relative shall be given by the department or the licensed child-placing agency only with the consent of the said natural parent or relative.[7]

From the state of Delaware: Subchapter I, 925, *Inspection of court records.*

> Anyone wishing to inspect any of the papers filed in connection with any adoption shall petition the Judge of the Superior Court concerning setting forth the reasons for inspection.[8]

From the state of Kansas: K.S.A. 65-2433. *Adoption Cases.*

> In all cases of adoption the state registrar, upon receipt of certified order of adoption shall prepare a supplementary certificate in the new name of the adopted person; and seal and file the original

certificate of birth with said certified copy attached thereto. Such sealed documents may be opened by the state registrar only upon demand of the adopted person if of legal age or an order of the court.[9]

From the state of New York: Domestic relations, Section 114. *Order of Adoption.*

No person shall be allowed access to such sealed records and order and any index thereof except upon an order of a judge or surrogate of the court in which the order was made or of a justice of the Supreme Court. No order for disclosure or access and inspection shall be granted except on good cause shown and on due notice to the adoptive parents and to such additional persons as the court may direct.[10]

To find out about the adoption laws in your state, you should contact your county's probate court, family court, or circuit court. These courts can be reached by looking under the county name in the telephone directory. The person for whom a searcher should ask varies from court to court. A good place to start is the clerk of the probate court.

Recognizing stages of the search and learning about adoption laws in your state are two important guidelines. Counting the cost of the search is another.

Keep within a Budget
From the beginning of the search effort, expenses will play an important part in how information can be gathered. Being aware of various expense categories will help in planning a budget.

Miscellaneous Fees
Costs will vary among the many public and private agencies that may be a part of a search. Copies of official certificates of record are held in state offices. These offices house birth, death, marriage, and divorce records. A birth certificate in one state may cost only two or three dollars; in another, the cost may be as high as fifteen dollars. Filing in a Probate Court to obtain records may run as high as a hundred dollars, as does registering in state reunion registries.

A number of states have a state mandated intermediary system, a system in which an agency or other group acts as the go-between for the searcher and his birth family. All states operate by different rules; fees can run between two hundred and two thousand dollars.

In the early stages of the search you may expect to pay to enter the registry, to obtain nonidentifying information, to petition the court, and perhaps, to enlist intermediary services. Some private adoption agencies may charge for opening and reviewing their files. Occasionally, hospitals and other institutions will charge to release information as do archives and public libraries. Usually this cost is low and is related to the cost of photocopying material.

Mailing Costs

Writing letters to gather information can run up the cost of the search rapidly. For example, Katherine Davis, sent 100 letters to members of her birth mother's high school graduating class with the hope that at least one person would know her married name. On another occasion she sent a certified letter to her birth father's last known address. By the time she had finally located her birth family members, she had spent well over $100 in postage alone. Learning how to gather valuable information from more specific sources would have reduced this cost.

Telephone Bills

Escalating phone bills slow down your search. Learning how to take advantage of time zone differences and special rates will help. Jayne Askin suggests other tips.

> In all cases, keep track of each person talked to. The person receiving the call might be a teenager or the spouse of the relative. Also, an unexpected call from the past might not immediately jog the memory or may catch someone off guard. When dealing with agencies, keeping track of the person spoken to will provide a referral record in any future exchange.[11]

Membership Dues in Support Organizations

Gaining needed support by joining an adoption, genealogical, or historical group will most likely require membership dues. These are legitimate fees that help defray the costs related to search assistance. Fees for these groups can vary from twenty-five to seventy-five dollars.

Factoring in the stage of your search, knowledge of state laws, and the cost for the search sets you on a solid foundation. Keeping track of information as it comes in is another necessity.

Document, Document, Document

Documenting information as it is collected is important, says Susan E. Friel-Williams, a search consultant in Boise, Idaho: "As the adoptee starts the search, she should sit down and write a biography on herself that includes date of birth, place, time, doctor, hospital, etc. After that, the adoptee should write another record on everything she has ever been told or has overheard about the adoption and/or biological parents. Most adoptees hear little things while growing up. Sometimes these bits of our history enable us to formulate the larger picture during the search."

Susan offers these specific suggestions:

- Purchase a three-ring binder or some other method of collecting paperwork and start a folder.
- Include in that folder "copies" of the original documentation that will be collected. This will include nonidentifying information, the amended birth certificate *and* any letters written to or received from agencies, hospitals, attorneys, etc.
- *Never* carry the original documentation anywhere. Make copies and leave one set in a safe place.
- Document every conversation—from the people you contact to the replies received.

"Often searchers get one clue from one person, another clue from someone else," Susan says. "Separately, those clues may appear to mean nothing, but if events and contacts were well-documented, eventually a person will be able to put them together into a very plausible scenario on the birth family. One of those little bits of information may be the missing puzzle piece that will enable the searcher to locate the person for whom he is looking."[12]

Learn Contact Strategies

Contact may be the most difficult part of the search process. It's important to determine if a letter or phone call will be the first mode of contact. Many factors play in this decision. The most important thing to remember is that *contact is the first impression after many years of separation!*

The following strategies were taken from material developed by Curry

Wolfe, a birth parents and search consultant, and are used with her permission.[13]

Letter or Phone Call?

The decision on whether to phone or write depends partly on the information you have been able to gain during the search. You may have the full address and phone number or just the address or phone number. Once the correct information is in hand, you can ask yourself a simple question: "How would I like to be contacted if the shoe were on the other foot?" Some people are phone people, others are letter people. There's a good chance your family member may have similar feelings.

There are many different views on the phone call versus the letter contact. There are no right or wrong answers to this question.

The phone call is a direct way of reaching the person and having an instant answer to the important questions. It allows you to hear your family member's voice. You get a true sense of how they feel about being contacted. Making a phone call enables you to make sure you have found the right person and no one else can intercept the call.

Wolfe offers these simple suggestions to prepare for the call:

1. Make the call at a reasonable time. Always be aware of time zone differences. Placing the call before 9:00 a.m. or after 9:00 p.m. is usually not a good idea. Contacting someone at work could create an extremely awkward situation. You should also avoid the dinner hour between 5:00 p.m. and 7:00 p.m.
2. Holiday calling, such as on Mother's Day, Father's Day, or Christmas may set up the adoptee for disappointment and hurt feelings. It could leave a sad memory of that holiday if the contact does not go well. Ordinary days are best.
3. Don't make the call alone; have someone there. Many times callers have become so overwhelmed and excited that they actually lose the ability to speak. Having someone to step in if necessary is helpful and it's nice to have someone there to talk to after the call.
4. Be prepared when making the phone call. Have some questions written down ahead of time to gain specific information, and leave blanks for taking notes.
5. When the correct person has been reached, speak clearly and slowly, but not unnaturally. Ask if they have time to talk privately because the discussion is of a personal nature. They will

most likely ask the caller's name at this time. Give them your complete name and phone number and ask that they write it down in case of a disconnection.

Now it's time to start into the "why" of the call. You may simply state the date and location of your birth. If this doesn't get an instant response, you will have to mention adoption. From this point on, the conversation will take on a life of its own.

If the receiver gets upset and doesn't wish to continue the call, understand that he or she may need some time to think things over. Offer to contact them at another time or to allow them to call back. Kindness and understanding are the words of the day. Never make promises you cannot keep. If the receiver is upset and doesn't want to be contacted again, don't make that promise. You will not be ready to give up so soon. Just be understanding and end the conversation for now.

If you don't feel comfortable making a phone call, a letter is a positive way of reaching out after many years of separation. The receiver is able to read the letter over and over and determine their most comfortable way of replying. And it becomes a keepsake forever.

While the letter doesn't produce as instant a reply as a phone call, it may be the best way of reaching out.

Writing a letter doesn't need to be an overwhelming task. Always keep in mind that it's the first contact in many years. This is not the time to express your sorrow and your needs.

The letter may be written in two ways. One way suggested by Betsie Norris is a vague, short style—an I'm Thinking of You card. "The card can read something like 'I'm thinking of you. We last saw each other on (give date of birth). My name has been changed to . . . and I can be reached at. . . .' This also protects some privacy if someone else finds the note," Betsie explains.

The other type of letter adds more detail. It doesn't need to be lengthy. It can be as short as four or five paragraphs. Curry Wolfe offers the following as a sample of the paragraphs and the kind of information you can express in this first contact.

1. Make the introduction in the first paragraph and include your name, date of birth, city and state. Then state your relationship to them.
2. The second paragraph is a good place to say why the letter was written. Keep it simple. Simply mention that you wish to learn

your medical and heritage information.

3. In the third paragraph you can offer some personal data. While this is not the time to tell your life story, you may wish to share briefly about education, family structure, and interests.

4. In the fourth paragraph state specifically what you are seeking. You may wish to ask for letters, phone conversations, pictures, or a possible reunion. Don't ask for too much at this point.

5. The closing paragraph should describe how you can be reached, the best times to call, and whether or not a collect call is acceptable. Selecting a closing word or phrase is difficult for many. Some choose Love, Sincerely, Always, or Yours forever. Choose what fits you best.

If there is no reply in a couple of weeks, wait at least one more week. The letter slows response time but offers the receiver time to process his or her reply. If you have not received a reply after three or four weeks, perhaps placing a phone call or simply writing a note stating the great importance of a reply will be helpful.

Being discreet, maintaining privacy, and not disclosing the whole story to everyone you contact is important. Avoid knocking on your family member's door without prior contact. It has been done, but confronting someone unannounced may start the reunion off on the wrong footing. This action may create tension that takes years to undo.

Many times a drive-by may be possible. If you are able to do this, don't stop and stare. Always keep in mind that others are not aware of the search. Be respectful on all accounts.

Plan Ahead for the Reunion

Adoptees spend a great deal of time and energy during the search process. Some plan well ahead, formulating plans on how, when, and where to make contact and eventually meet. Others, caught up in the intensive nature of the process, fail to make such plans. One adoptee commented, "I didn't make plans on how to meet because I guess in the back of my mind I didn't think it would happen. I was surprised and completely thrown into a whirlwind because I hadn't thought this part of the process through."

Planning ahead is crucially important. According to Mary Jo Rillera, author of *The Adoption Searchbook*, there are several specific aspects to consider:

1. *Where will the reunion take place?* Deciding if the reunion will

take place in the adoptee's home or birth parent's home or in a restaurant or office is an important decision. It should be a neutral point where each person feels comfortable and has the opportunity to limit the time together should the emotional need arise.

2. *Who will participate in the reunion?* Making a decision about who will be part of the initial reunion is critical. It depends on several factors—how much prior contact through mail or on the phone there has been, how comfortable a person is in larger groups, and how intense the first contacts were. It's important to get time alone with the newfound person. If the reunion takes place in a group, taking a walk together or finding another way to be alone is important.

3. *When will the reunion take place?* Deciding on a meeting time will be dictated by the geographical location to each other and the daily schedules of all involved. A meeting should be planned where time pressure is not a factor. There should be some correspondence or phone contact prior to the physical meeting.[14]

Be Prepared for Anything

Some adoptees who have reported rejection said that acknowledging the possibility of rejection to friends in a support group helped them deal with the eventual reality. The cases of rejection reported in various studies are less than 10 percent.[15] In discussing the possibility of initial rejection, Mary Jo Rillera comments that some contacts result in denial by the sought parties that they are the correct people or that they have any knowledge of what the adoptee is suggesting. Occasionally the found person abruptly withdraws and refuses further contact. Rillera advises the adoptee to make sure he has documented the search thoroughly so that he doesn't doubt earlier conclusions. Second, make sure there's a way to write or call the found person in the future. There have been many cases where, within a short time, both parties have handled their fears, dealt with resurfaced pain, or realized what the contact really meant.[16]

The First Contact—What It Was Like for Others

Initiating the first contact is an emotionally tense moment. A wide range of experiences confront adoptees at this point of the search and reunion. For some, the outcome may be positive, warm, and inviting. On the other hand, the fallout may be rejecting, painful, and crushing. What do those who have crossed this bridge say about their experiences?

Beyond My Wildest Fantasies

Though I fantasized the reunion would be perfect, I never really believed it would be as beautiful and passionate as it was—and still is. Meeting Mary (my birth mother) has brought a sense of wholeness to me. I never knew what it meant to feel complete. Now I do. In addition to finding her, I found three half-sisters, a grandmother, and a whole mess of aunts, uncles, and cousins. That has taken some getting used to.
—Carol Wallenfelsz, age 23

Rough at First

Learn as much as you can before you jump in not knowing how deep the water is. I thought I was prepared, but my first contact did not go well and I was absolutely devastated. I thought I was ready for anything, and I probably was prepared as well as I could have been. I had been a member of a search/support group for three years prior to finding my birth mother and making the initial contact. I strongly urge people to join a support group before making contact. The knowledge you attain through other people's experiences is absolutely invaluable in these situations. Luckily, my birth mother had a chance to think things over and called me back six days later. Now I feel that I'm forming relationships that will be in my life forever. Everyone in my birth mother's family (including my full-blooded brother and sister) is embracing me with open arms and unconditional love.
—Mary Meaker, age 28

An Awesome Experience

It was breathtaking to look at my mirror image with whom I share many personality traits and realize this was really happening. I gained three (so far) very nice friends and/or relatives, knowing there are more I have not yet had the pleasure of meeting.
—Beverly Perry, 34

Unexpected Anguish

I ignored advice to be prepared for anything—including rejection. I didn't allow myself to believe rejection would be part of my own journey. I just don't understand why my birth mother has no interest in even talking with me on the phone. What is so difficult about that? When I mailed the first letter, the reply came back: "Don't try to contact me ever again. You were part of my past." I have gone through such incredible periods of depression. What is she afraid of? Maybe she never told anyone about me.
—Carolyn Miller, age 34

I Feel Like a Different Person

The result of my search has been a reunion with my birth mother and two half-brothers. I have even met my grandfather. All have welcomed me with open arms and hearts and we continue to have an ongoing and growing relationship that keeps getting better every day. I feel like the missing piece of me has now been put back into place and I am a whole person once again.
—Shelly McKinney, age 32

A MOTHER'S LOVE
May 16, 1986
Dear Betsie,

Your call has brought us such joy. I can't begin to express myself. I've written hundreds of letters to you in my heart over the years and was particularly with you for each birthday and special celebration as I perceived it—nursery school, first day of kindergarten, graduation, etc.

I can imagine your joy at not only finding me, but also your natural father and full-blood brothers. I have wished for you so often, but have strongly felt that what was done at your birth was done out of strong love for you and our desire for you to have a normal family situation, which we could not provide at that time. . . .

We have so many questions that we can't ask them all now. What do you like? Where did you go to grade school, high school; you mentioned Maine? How did you like it? How did you choose nursing? Do you like animals and on and on and on. We'll save some. We'll see you soon.

Much love,

You'll have to decide what to call us. Whatever you decide is okay. (From the first letter from Betsie's birth mother)

The end of the search for many adoptees brings a sense of completion, an intense perception of connectedness. Found answers. Found people. Planned reunions. However, for another segment of the adult adoptee population, discovering the harsh realities of a history of abuse, the death of a birth parent, or rejection moves them only to more questions, perhaps more pain. Yet the discoveries are not without hope. It can move them to a greater depth of self-examination, emotional growth, and spiritual awareness.

CHAPTER SIX

FACING A HISTORY OF ABUSE OR NEGLECT

---------------- ✛ ----------------

The need to search is not about

looking for only happy outcomes—

it is about finding the truth.

BETSIE NORRIS

Kathy, age twenty-nine, has very few friends. She stays at home, seldom venturing out. She calls her husband, Jeremy, at work at least three times a day, just to make sure he is there. Jeremy has tired of the smothering he feels from Kathy and is thinking about what to do about it. The more she envelops him, the more he withdraws. The more he withdraws, the tighter she clings.

Kathy is the product of an abusive/neglectful family of origin. Memories of being locked in a bedroom as her parents left the children for endless hours remain vivid and frightening. At the age of five, she was removed from her birth home. She lived in three foster homes before her adoption by a family at the age of eight. She was separated from three other siblings, one older and two younger.

Kathy's early recollection of childhood was devoid of feeling safe and being able to trust. These issues still haunt her in adulthood. She knows she's in trouble, and she wonders if finding her birth family would help her to stabilize emotionally.

Richard is what is commonly called a "workaholic." At thirty-three, he owns his own business and works sixteen hours a day. He's obsessed with the need to succeed. He wants to completely eradicate memories of what it was like to have absolutely nothing to eat or anything clean to wear. Displaced from his birth family because of severe physical neglect when seven years of age and adopted soon after, Richard still vividly recalls empty cabinets, an empty refrigerator, and the deep gnawing of hunger. He will never forget the day his mother left him with a friend with a promise to return. She never did. He's so determined to overcome his past that he's in danger of losing something in his present—his wife and children.

As an adult child of a severely dysfunctional family, Richard is still controlled by the images imprinted on his young mind. He suffers shame and embarrassment about his past. He refuses to talk openly about it, denying its grip on him. Lately, when alone and afraid, he considers, "Maybe a journey back to meet them would free me to live life in a better way."

Walking out on her third marriage, Lisa struggles with intense feelings of loneliness, depression, and emptiness. Her three marriages were a vain attempt to fill up the hollowness that consumed her. Yet fear of intimacy and an inability to express herself blocked growth and eventually led to disillusionment and abandonment.

Throughout her early childhood Lisa was a victim of physical, sexual, and emotional abuse. Taken into foster care at age six, she was eventually placed for adoption at age nine. Even at that young age, she vowed never to trust or love another family.

Because of her pain at the hands of her abusive birth father and her emotionally absent mother, she spends all her energy longing for those elusive words "I love you" from the people who hurt her. "Maybe," she ponders, "if I can find them, maybe now they will love me."

Adults who entered their adoptive homes as older children usually carry with them memories of people and places. They also cart along a history of physical, emotional, or sexual abuse or neglect. Some choose to ignore the effects of such raw early life experiences. However, for most, escape is nearly impossible.

In his book, *Adult Children of Abusive Parents*, Steven Farmer comments,

> The abuse suffered in childhood continues to substantially affect them. They long for a break from their cycles of repetitious, self-defeating patterns of behavior, yet they cling to familiar habits because they know no other way. Conflict and struggle dominate their lives as do persistent feelings of being victimized, exploited, and betrayed by others.[1]

Most adults who were victims of abuse carry no outward signs; there are no broken legs or arms, only wounded spirits. Many talk of moving into adulthood under the cloud of anxiety, depression, low self-esteem, and chronic loneliness. Unconsciously, they continue to be controlled by the faint memories of a painful past. They are simply unaware that their present difficulties most likely are intricately tied to the trauma of a lost childhood.

Marian Parker, a veteran adoption social worker in Ohio, has encountered many struggling adult adoptees from abusive backgrounds. "Self-doubt becomes a real issue for these young adults," Parker said. "Being placed for adoption and dealing with thoughts of 'What's wrong with me, I was given up' is compounded with the feelings of knowing that one was abused or neglected as well. They think to themselves, 'It's worse than not being wanted; they hurt me besides.'"[2]

Why do many adults, adopted as older children with a background of abuse and neglect, choose to take the journey back? How does an adult, adopted as an older child, move beyond the maze of emotional pain created from his abusive past? It's a journey not easily undertaken. The first step is to find out as much factual information as possible. A second step is to become aware of silent, hidden issues created by the past that may have an impact on emotional well-being. A third step toward healing from a broken past compels the adult to examine what to expect if a reunion with the family of origin takes place. Finally, the adoptee must ask and answer a difficult question—"How do I know I'm ready for this?"

WHY SOME GO BACK

According to Kay Donley Ziegler, trainer/consultant for National Resource Center for Special Needs Adoption, almost all adults adopted as older children have thought about trying to piece their life together. "The thoughts of searching are universal. They are normal," she said. "Some think about it. Some talk about it. Others take action, pushing on in an attempt to find some resolution to their pain."

"I believe," Kay continues, "that for these adults, it is an issue of closure as to why they return. They are trying to figure out what happened to them and why. They have perhaps grown up with a sense that they were at fault for the abuse—they had something to do with causing the family problem. They wonder about being defective—imperfect. Going back and finding out what happened enables many to put it into the right context."[3]

For many, facing the events of their past becomes an absolute necessity to finding emotional stability.

A Walking Time Bomb

Until now, Michael, in his early twenties, has pretended that his adoptive parents were his birth parents. He deliberately crammed away memories of his alcoholic father's violent outbursts and the sight of his mother cowering in a corner of the room. He refused to talk about his birth parents, even to acknowledge their existence. However, incredible anxiety stalks him, making him feel like a time bomb ready to explode. He finally admits that perhaps his emotional problems are related to a past he tried to erase.

Dr. Randolph Severson, an adoption counselor with Hope Cottage in Dallas, Texas, sees this similar scenario.

Many come to me as adults saying they feel like a time bomb ready to go off. This happens often in those who were under the age of six when the abuse or trauma occurred.

They have not seen their family of origin since that time and because of their young age, they do not have any context for relating to those persons outside the memory of the abuse.

Life is a continuum of human experience and the abusive event was so overpowering it is their only memory from which they can develop a sense of identity from a historical context.

As these adults move through adolescence and attempt to develop self-image from their historical context, two issues present themselves. First, they don't have much memory to serve them and second, what memory they do have is often traumatic and even horrifying.[4]

Defusing the Time Bomb

Kathy, Richard, and Lisa all made a decision to address the clicking time bomb in their lives by seeking the help of a professional capable of addressing the memories of their painful past. The role of such a professional in preparing an adult adoptee to face the past and make future connections is vital. How this individual helps the adoptee to walk through these issues is pivotal to a successful recovery.

"When I can," Dr. Severson says, "I work to get into the historical context of the person's memory. No one person abused a child twenty-four hours a day. I try to help this person recover any memory, however small it may be, that is positive." Another step in a therapeutic approach moves the adoptee toward healing and resolution. Severson adds:

> Using what I call "explaining therapy," that is, giving them as much information as possible, is a successful tool. That information includes such things as factors that contribute to the intergenerational patterns of abuse, social/economic influences, and the psychological make-up of the family of origin. Fifty to sixty percent of my work is explaining therapy. Going back to an agency and getting as much information as is relevant to them is essential.[5]

When Kathy returned to the child welfare agency that had been involved with her family situation, she was met by a caseworker who understood the value of giving her as much information as possible. Dealing with the touchy subject of needing identifying information wasn't an issue for Kathy. She had known her original name and the names of most birth family members all her life. What she needed were the facts about what happened.

Kathy found that the image she carried in her mind of lazy, irresponsible birth parents who sat around in a filthy house was basically incorrect. What she did find was that her birth mother was a young woman in her early twenties of somewhat limited capabilities. Her birth father, a product of a severely dysfunctional family was overwhelmed with the incredible responsibilities of raising four children when he himself was not much more than a child. Abuse was the only way he knew how to control their behavior. Neither parent had any concept of how to provide a nurturing, safe environment. With each day, the load grew heavier. Out of desperation, with no help or positive future in sight, Kathy's birth father abandoned the family. Her birth mother was incapable of carrying on. The authorities stepped in.

When Kathy learned through "explaining therapy" the events and circumstances of her birth family, she experienced an unexpected and overwhelming sense of relief.

"One main reason I hold on so tightly to Jeremy," Kathy realized, "is that I never felt worthy of being loved. I didn't want to lose out again. I thought we must have been pretty terrible kids for someone to dump us. Now I'm beginning to understand a little of what pushed them to do what they did. I feel freer to work on the issues from my past that are controlling the present and will interrupt my future."

Kathy did not find a fairy-tale ending. She found something far more important—the truth.

"The truth is paramount for searching adoptees," Marian Parker says, "no matter what is found. Finding out answers is immensely important, because what fantasies exist for the adoptee may be far worse than the truth that may have been magnified by secrecy."

Looking into the historical context of one's circumstances is part of the healing process for adults adopted as older children. Another piece of the picture is to look at the hidden, silent issues that surface when faced with the question of reunion.

Issues That Surface as Reunion Thoughts Emerge
After Richard faced his past, hidden feelings that were directly related to his early life experiences emerged. Others adopted as older children, like Richard, speak of similar emotions and thoughts. What feelings do these adults uncover as they choose to face people and places from another time?

"Why Was I Rescued?" *—Survivor's Guilt*
Part of a family of five children, Lauranna Benedict carries with her the knowledge that she was "rescued" from an abusive home environment and that three of her sisters were not.

> I was about three and a half, the fourth child of five, when the authorities placed all of us into foster care. My parents were given time to get their lives together, I am told. After three years, the

court decided they could have three of us back—my three older sisters. My brother and I were placed together in an adoptive home. I was six when that happened.

Now as an adult, I've learned that things did not go well with my three sisters. I look back with incredible guilt. I was raised free from abuse. I had the opportunity to go to college and make something of myself. I have trouble allowing myself to feel good about my life. Right now, I feel sorrow for them and wonder, "Why was I spared?"

Ronny Diamond, Director of Post Adoption Services for Spence Chapin Services to Families and Children in New York, works with adults who deal with abuse issues and are considering initiating a reunion with birth family members.

"One of the concerns I see these young adults carry is what I call 'survivor's guilt,'" Diamond offered. "There's a sense of relief that they were rescued from an injurious home environment on the one hand, but guilt for leaving on the other. They ask themselves 'If I could have stayed, could I have helped them?' They feel this especially if other siblings were left at home. Some even go so far as to think their leaving left the family in far worse shape and they should be blamed."[6]

Closely related to survivor's guilt is another issue that looms overhead. It comes from a message the adoptee received from his birth parents.

"You'll Be Back Someday"—*An Obligation to Rescue*

The scene remains frozen in Benjamin's mind. Although now twenty-three years old, he still remembers the day, at age seven, when he said goodbye to his mother. He recalls the blue dress she was wearing, the hole in the toe of her shoe, and her disheveled hair. Most of all he recalls what she said to him. "Someday, Benje, you'll be back. They're taking you now, but someday you'll be back and you can take care of me then. I know you will be back." That memory drives his need to find his mother.

A message often given to older children by their birth parents prior to the final separation is simply, "You must come back; I know you will."

Nancy Ward, a senior social worker at the Children's Home Society of Minnesota, says this farewell experience sends two profound messages to the vulnerable youngster, which he jams deep into the back pocket of his mind to retrieve at a later date.

The first message is an extreme obligation to his birth parent to reconnect. For some, it goes beyond the faint promises made by a frightened child, mushrooming into a driving, motivating force—*a vow that cannot be broken.*

The second message of unrelenting obligation is the need to rescue the birth parents. "There's a perception," Ward explains, "that the birth parents need to be rescued. Some have created a fantasy of 'the poor people who lost their children.' These adults deny the reality of the abuse and neglect. This idealization of their birth parents propels them toward reunion."[7]

"Maybe This Is Who I Really Am"—Identity and Feelings of Shame
Both Ronny Diamond and Nancy Ward in counseling adoptees walk with them on a rocky, thorny path as they grapple with a sense of who they really are.

"I think an adopted person's roots in his biological family are no different for a child who has been placed at birth or as an older child," Diamond asserts. "It's still a question of 'Who am I—what is my identity?'"

Diamond feels that many adoptees whose wound is the product of physical, emotional, or sexual abuse carry a deep sense of shame. They say to themselves, *This is part of who I am.* They wonder, *How far away from being like them am I really? Can I surpass them? If I want to reconnect, do I have to become what they are and not absorb the values of my adoptive parents?*

For many, a wrestling match of the heart and soul takes place as the battle to define themselves continues. They wonder who they will become.

Mitch Walters, now twenty-five, recalls the struggles he felt in late adolescence as he attempted to discover who he was and what he would become in relation to his birth family and adoptive family.

> I was adopted at the age of six and I still have memories of a pretty rough home environment. When I was a teen, I wondered just how hard I should try in life. If I wanted to be like my birth family, it wouldn't require much effort. If I wanted to identify with my adoptive family, it would pull out the best I could do. I felt that reconnecting with my birth mother and birth family members would fill in an identity gap for me. It did help me to define what I had become with the help and support of my adoptive parents. I didn't particularly respect the lifestyle of my birth family and made a decision that I wanted more out of life than that. I still see them maybe once or twice a year, but the visits are short and tense.

Stacking the emotional shelves of life with such issues as survivor guilt, obligations, and identity questions gets further complicated by the feelings created by one more issue, perhaps the most controlling and destructive one.

94

"Do I Dare Feel It?"—Acknowledging and Resolving Anger

Barbara Getterings, age thirty-three, recollects all too well what it felt like
to hear the back door swing open and hear the blustery, angry rantings of
her violent, abusive father. She remembers all too well the many occasions,
after his fits of rage, that all members of the family had to pretend as if nothing happened. No one could be sad. No one could be scared. And, of
course, no one could be angry.

> My birth father would come home from work usually drunk. It was
> like a tornado hit the front room. He would just blow the place
> apart, leaving us in the wake, physically in pain and emotionally
> traumatized. I learned early in life to be afraid of anger because it
> was so connected to violence.
>
> I went *inside* with my anger, where it rotted over time but never
> went away. As I grew older, that anger rose to the surface as depres-
> sion and substance abuse. I finally got help and learned that I could
> openly express the rage I had buried for so long. I want to see my
> birth father again; I was ten the last time I saw him. But I will see
> him as a healthier person than I used to be. I now know how to be
> liberated from the anger that so consumed me.

For many adults adopted as older children, anger is not only the product of the abuse that took place in the family of origin, but is further complicated by the deep pain of separation from birth family members. What
to do with that anger is the next question. Author Dwight Wolter, who also
experienced an abusive dysfunctional family, shared valuable insights as he
resolved his anger.

> I began to enjoy the expression of anger. Anger, sarcasm, and wit
> make a potent combination. The adrenaline my anger released had
> a druglike effect. My heart beat fast. My blood flowed quickly. My
> face was flushed and, best of all, I felt right! Look at the way I was
> raised. No one could deny me the right to be angry. Anger became
> the fuel that propelled me through difficult situations. Anger
> became the passion that let me know I was alive.
>
> . . . Then I realized that it was not getting angry but remaining
> angry that had become a problem for me. If someone hurt me, I
> would get angry instead of feeling the pain. It was difficult to let go
> of my attraction to anger. . . . I want to wear my anger like a suit of
> armor to spare me from pain. But I can't. Now I'm losing my anger

about never having had a childhood. What I'm left with is sadness. And facing sadness is not easy. All of my life I would rather have been dragged across a field of boulders by wild horses than feel the immense sadness within me. Anger was so much easier to feel.[8]

Emotional issues of guilt, obligation, shame, and anger, if left unattended, can sprout like weeds within the life of an adult with a disturbing past, choking off growth, emotional health, and quality relationships. Choosing to rip out the festering weeds with the help of support groups or counseling will enable the adoptee to manage whatever comes as a result of the reunion. Dealing with expectations of a reunion in the light of reality then becomes possible.

Dealing with Expectations

What can adoptees expect to find when making plans to reunite with birth family members whose abuse or neglect has left painful memories? Marian Parker suggests, "Be ready for *anything*. Be prepared for the worst possible outcome or maybe a positive encounter. There is just no way to know."

Dr. Randolph Severson makes several more observations.

First, the human mind tends to freeze a person in our minds just as we remember them. We forget that life goes on. People may change, and of course, they may not either. They have to be able to move that person on in time. Often the abusive family is made up of young parents overwhelmed financially and emotionally. As the years have passed, they have matured and gotten on top of the early problems. I caution those who are searching and making contact that the people they will meet are not going to be the same people they were twenty years ago or like they remember, if there is a memory. They may find a person who has incredible guilt over the past and feels great remorse. They may find a person living in denial of any responsibility and even refusing to discuss the past.

Ronny Diamond agrees with Dr. Severson. The memory is frozen in time—on both sides. "Often the work of the adoptee in considering expectations," Diamond interjects, "is to look at the range of possibilities. On one end of the continuum they may find the family with their act together, which causes them to ask the question, 'If you did it now, why not then?' On the other end of the continuum they may find the parents still strung out. It validates the history but keeps the door to reentering their lives closed. Either discovery creates conflicting feelings."

Another possibility adoptees may find as they return to their birth parents is a "revised history." Adoptees must be aware of the strong possibility that when they seek the "hows and whys" of what happened, their birth family may not come clean, according to Kay Donley Ziegler.

"A person who slips back into his abuse history may find a parent who denies that history, maybe out of pride, maybe out of shame, or maybe from a pathological refusal to face the truth," Kay explains. "The problem with going back is that a vast majority of the pieces may be filtered through a revisionary process and one may unearth only remnants of the truth."

Confronting the historical context of their lives, facing issues, and processing expectations prepare the adoptee to reconnect with his birth family. Yet how does a person know she is emotionally, psychologically, and spiritually ready for such a meeting?

How to Know If You're Ready

Michelle Conover, now twenty-seven, made a decision to find and reconnect with her birth family. She had been removed due to severe neglect. All of her adult life she had wondered why her birth parents couldn't get their lives together. How could she know if she was ready to see them again?

"One of the initial factors I look at when counseling adoptees on readiness," Ronny Diamond says, "is what their process has been up to now—what work the adoptee has done emotionally. Have they taken a few steps, stopped and processed, and begun again? Or are they impulsive and quick acting? I then urge them to slow down.

"I also ask them 'future' questions like *What are your concerns? How do you feel about those concerns and how do you think you will feel about them in six months or next year? What impact do you expect it to have on your life if you meet your family?* All these are important issues to filter through one's present life situation."

Dr. Severson also feels that readiness must be assessed before an encounter. "One of the questions I ask myself in dealing with an adult adoptee in this circumstance is, Do they have enough life experience and enough self-knowledge to forgive? If the answer is no, I am pessimistic about the reunion. If the answer is yes, I am much more optimistic."

Why are life experiences so important at this stage of the reunion process? According to Severson, "Life experiences create a judgmental system that can work for or against a positive reunion outcome. Here's one of the key life experience factors I look for: Is this person a parent? If they are, they probably know something about parental rage.

"I also look for life experiences that have prevented a 'black and white' judgmental perspective—How could anyone do that to a child?—and encouraged more of a gray perspective—a willingness to look at the abusive person's whole life context."

Life experiences create the ability to forgive, another important dynamic to a successful meeting, Severson feels. For many adopted persons trying to bridge the gap from the past to the present, the ability to look beyond the memory to forgiveness unlocks the door housing rage, bitterness, and resentment. Dwight Wolter knows something of that journey.

The process of forgiveness might *begin* by looking at our parents, but it always *ends* by looking at ourselves. Forgiveness is more about us than it is about them.

Many of us who were raised in dysfunctional homes use unforgiveness and resentment as a means of keeping away our true feelings. By focusing on our parents' failings, we don't have to look at our own character defects. Rage, fear, and anger lurk within an unforgiving heart. To forgive implies a willingness to admit that our old ways of dealing with our parents don't work anymore. We sense a need for change but are unsure of how to go about it. After a lifetime of focusing on our parents, it might feel terribly selfish to consider our own welfare first. We may feel we will once again open ourselves to the same abuse we were subjected to as children. . . . We stare at *an image* of our parents until our eyes hurt. We probe their lives more than our own because it might be much more painful to turn our eyes around and look into ourselves. We may claim it's not that we aren't willing to forgive but that they don't deserve it. Sometimes we might believe they deserve to be forgiven. Sometimes we would still rather focus on what we believe our parents might be forgiven for than on our own ability (or inability) to forgive.[9]

THE JOURNEY TOWARD FORGIVENESS

Randy Hopkins spent a portion of her earliest years in an abusive home and in an orphanage prior to adoption. The issues discussed above moved her to unravel an unknown past. Her story is one of pain, confusion, discovery, and forgiveness.

As I entered adolescence, damaging thoughts took root in my heart and mind. I convinced myself that since my family life was different from anyone's that I knew, I wasn't as good as the rest of my friends. Tremendous feelings of inadequacy barred me from trying new things or from branching out into friendships.

By the time I was nineteen, I was still plagued by feelings of deep resentment. I had a lot of anger toward the parents who had abused me as a two-year-old. I became more and more bitter all the time. I don't know how many times I thought to myself, *Mom and Dad, you left me. You were never there for me.*

I felt stuck in a downward spiral of negativism that drained me of happiness and peace. I had to put the fragmented pieces of my life together. I know that from the beginning, my search was directed by God, for it was just a matter of weeks before I located many family members.

Like many adopted kids, I manufactured fantasies about my birth parents. I hoped to see them as wealthy people who deeply regretted giving me away. As I stood on the front porch of a small house that summer day, looking at the disheveled woman who had given birth to me, all sorts of emotions welled up within me. I spent three hours with her. Our conversation was empty and strained. What I heard and saw jarred me to reality. It was obvious that alcohol still permeated this home, just as I had been told. When I walked out the door, I left my fantasies behind.

The process of healing began that day as I encountered the desperate, tragic state of my birth family. Their lives were empty— ravaged by alcohol, drug abuse, and poverty. God had spared me such a life.

Compassion filled me. I did forgive those who had left me with so many missing pieces. Now I could freely go on with my life, stronger with the reality of what my life has become.[10]

For many years, adoptees have—some with courage, some with timidity—reconnected with their birth family members after years of separation. For some the encounter was positive and restorative. For some it was flat and emotionless, as if trying to resurrect something that had long ago died. For others, the heartache of seeing continuing devastation brought grief but liberating truth as well.

I Still Loved Him

I was adopted when I was ten years old. When I turned twenty-one, I wanted to go back and find my dad. When we met, it was really weird, it

was like I had only been gone a short time. I didn't know what to do with what I felt—should I trust him? I did know that I still had some love left in me for him.
—Shane Patrick, age 24

I Thought They Would Care

When I turned eighteen, I remember announcing to my adoptive parents that it was time to go back and live with my birth family. I was separated from them when I was seven. My adoptive mother wisely told me to do what I needed to do, their door would always be open. I found my birth mother only an hour away. I thought she would care about seeing me. She didn't. I thought I would have deep feelings about being with her. I didn't. It was like nothing was left. After staying with her for a few weeks, I called my parents and asked to come home. I hoped they would care. They did.
—Michelle Michaels, age 25

I Felt Only Pity

From the time I was seven years old, I vowed I would return to my birth family. I just knew in my heart that by then they would be a happy family doing well and glad to see me. After finally finding them, my fantasy was shattered. My alcoholic father stumbled to the door and struggled to find a memory of me. My mother had died, also a victim of alcohol. I couldn't feel anger, just pity at the tragedy of their lives. At least now I knew the truth and it was just like I was told.
—Justin Brown, age 29

If you came from an abusive family of origin, it's important to keep an open mind during your search. Remember that just as you have changed over the years, your birth family has changed too. Hopefully this change has been for the better. But keep in mind that you are an adult now; you have a lot more choices and control than you did years ago. Your future can be as positive as you want it to be.
—Betsie Norris, age 34

Dealing with Special Issues Within the Search

---✦---

CHAPTER SEVEN

A WALK INTO THE WILDERNESS: LEARNING OF YOUR ADOPTION AS AN ADULT

❖

If I had not had my identity

anchored in my relationship with

God, this would have been a much

more devastating crisis, because my

human identity has been destroyed.

LOIS RABEY, AGE 49

To keep a secret from someone is to block information or evidence from reaching that person and to do so intentionally. To keep a secret is to make a value judgment, for whatever reason, that it's not that person's right to possess the secret. To keep a secret requires a maze built by concealment, disguises, camouflage, whispers, silence, or lies.

- Lois Rabey, at forty-seven, discovered the secret as she sat by the bedside of her elderly father.
- Jan Campbell, at forty-four, discovered the secret in a casual conversation with a relative on a family vacation.
- Moya Baker, at fifty, discovered the secret when her brother found his amended birth certificate and began to ask questions.
- Tammy Pasela, at thirty-four, discovered the secret from her sister who sat at the deathbed of her mother.
- Sharon Slagle, at thirty-two, discovered the secret while enjoying a conversation with a distant cousin.
- Alissa Whitman, at twenty-eight, discovered the secret because a family member let it slip.

Each of these individuals stumbled onto life-altering secrets after personal identities were formed, adult relationships secured, and heritages passed on to future generations. Each represents thousands of other adoptees who grew up in the shadow of the secret. One day, at the most unlikely time, each heard the same disturbing words—"You were adopted."

This revelation changed the course of their lives. It was a secret that redefined present relationships and a dilemma that added new people and places and enlarged a family system. It was a mysterious disclosure that sent many wandering into an emotional, psychological, and spiritual wilderness. It was a crisis of the whole person—mind, body, and soul. It would require responses from the depths of their souls that would eventually, hopefully, lead to inward resolution and outward reconciliation.

THE CONSPIRACY OF SILENCE[1]

For many adopted persons in mid-life and beyond, the fact of their adoption was hidden in an attempt to deny its reality. For many adoptive parents of the 1940s, 1950s, and 1960s, this secrecy was a misguided decision encouraged by the paradigm of the time. Yet this action gave no thought to the long-term future of the adoptee or insight into what the consequences of such secrecy would do.

"While some secrets can bring people together by giving them a sense of intimacy and sharing," says author Betty Jean Lifton, "secrets can be destructive if they cause shame and guilt, prevent change, render one powerless, or hamper one's sense of reality."[2] Adoption, in the last half of the twentieth century, became that pathogenic type of secret requiring a conspiracy of silence to maintain it.

"Finding out the secret of one's adoption as an adult feels like absolute betrayal," says Dr. Dirck Brown, family therapist and author. "It is the most prominent, deepest sense of betrayal. It is a real blow, a psychological injury."[3]

Although the adoptee knows nothing of his family status, extended family members often do. Psychologist Mark Parel calls this type of secret the *internal* secret, which a few family members keep from another family member.[4] Even if the adoptive parents ably maneuvered through the maze of concealment with disguises, silence, or lies, a careless comment by a relative, the discovery of hidden papers in the back of a dresser drawer, or the reading of a will brought the secret to light.

"There are far more people who learn of their adoptive status at the deathbed of a parent or the settling of an estate than the general public has any idea," comments Dr. Randolph Severson. "When the truth comes out, an emotional rippling effect takes over."[5]

What Dr. Severson has observed in counseling adoptees experiencing this personal crisis is that there is both absolute shock and relief.

"More people suspect it but have not admitted it, or they are unconsciously aware of it," Severson explains. "There were probably subtle hints along the way, such as a lack of pictures during pregnancy or coming home from the hospital. There were probably no stories unless they were fabricated. Some have resurrected memories of whispers at family reunions and holiday get-togethers.

"As the shock subsides, relief comes when the adopted person realizes what he thought was off base wasn't. These adults have grown up wondering, Why do people get anxious when I talk about my birth? Why don't I look like anyone? Why do I get strange looks when this subject comes up? As the truth emerges, there is a rhythm of shock, anger, and relief."

She Wondered All Her Life

Lois Rabey, now forty-nine, grew up an only child feeling very wanted and loved. Occasionally she would hear her mother say, "We couldn't have any children and then you came along," but the phrase had no real meaning to her.

Occasionally the kids in the neighborhood teased her saying, "You're adopted, you're adopted." A quick run home to a reassuring remark from her mother, "No honey, you're not, and if you were you would be special and chosen," calmed her fears. These statements and many more scattered throughout her childhood were the hidden remnants of a part of Lois's legitimate personhood, her true identity. It wasn't until her elderly father let the secret slip that Lois was able to gather those mysterious pieces of her childhood together and some of the painful issues in her life began to make sense.

Looking back on her life after the adoption revelation, Lois recounts memories of her parents' behavior that were a part of the secret they felt constrained to keep.

"I can remember my mother standing and watching out the window for long periods of time as if she were looking for someone. They were both paranoid about privacy and had a very guarded attitude about their personal life. My only babysitter when I was young was my grandmother." It was as if her parents lived in fear that Lois would someday be reclaimed.

Not only did Lois's parents guard her and their personal life, her father demanded something further. It was as if he could never accept the fact that Lois was theirs only by the bond of adoption, not by blood.

"As I grew older, the primary situation that caused tension—an escalating tension on my father's part—was that he needed to be reflected in me," Lois recalls. "He had to see himself in me. It was an obsession for him that I be like him and think like him. As a teenager, my faith became a vital reality to me. He wanted me to forget about it. He was relentless with an ongoing verbal violation of my personal boundaries.

"There was a constant attempt on his part to change me. I never went through a rebellion as a teen; I tried to be a people pleaser. Now I see that my role growing up was to keep my dad from being angry. It was an incredible pressure to be the go-between with my parents. Life was a constant tap dance."

As Lois grew into adulthood, and after the sudden death of her mother, she became even more keenly aware of the unhealthy nature of her relationship with her father. But she had no clue as to what could be the problem.

"After my mother died July 4, 1990, I found myself saying, 'I cannot grow up. I can't go on.' My relationship with my father felt like a rubber band that kept us attached. I went into counseling to help sort out the blockage I felt with him. I did everything the counselor suggested to break his hold on me, but there was something, a heavy black cloud, that I couldn't see through."

In 1992, Lois's eighty-four-year-old father became extremely ill—a fast moving case of dementia—and he was moved to a nursing home. As Lois visited with her father, each time she entered the room he would ask the same question, "Are you adopted?" Puzzled, she finally contacted an uncle she had not seen since she was ten years old. He confirmed the truth, as did other relatives and friends of her parents. For Lois, the revelation brought instant relief. It also left in its wake shock and emotional upheaval. It propelled her into the wilderness, a dry barren place of the unknown.

"When I learned of my adoption, it brought a tremendous sense of relief—emotionally and physically. Most of my adult life I discerned something was amiss, and this explained it all. It explained the actions of my parents. It explained the harshness and demands of my father and the incredible hold he had on me." This knowledge brought relief, but it also brought shock.

"I was incredibly shocked that Mother never told me. I felt close to her. But I understand why she did it. I think it was my mother's desire to be a wonderful mother. She died in my arms right after a heart attack. As we were frantically waiting for the ambulance, I administered CPR. I kept thinking, "You gave me life, let me do this for you. It's a tragedy, for her sake, that she died never revealing the truth."

Although Lois has yet to experience a great deal of anger, she believes "the anger isn't over for me yet. I don't handle anger well and the focus has been on absorbing the shock.

"On one hand, I feel like I'm in transition. I know what the truth is. The horrible tension is gone. I've had conversations with Dad and told him I knew. He wept and there was a lot of healing that happened for me.

"On the other hand, I have questions . . . I feel a sense of abandonment. I feel like the whole world is on the inside of a glass and I'm on the outside. My prevailing emotional feeling is that everybody marches along to a family rhythm and I don't know what mine is, and now it's too late. I should have counted somewhere enough to be told the truth."

When Lois learned of her adoption, she felt like she'd been thrown into the undertow of a fast moving river. However, this time she had a life preserver—the truth. It validated what she felt deep in her heart many years ago. The truth rescued her.

Jan Always Suspected It

Discovering the secret of her adoption at age forty-four confirmed for Jan Campbell a lifetime of suspicion.

"The reality, of course, never hit me as a child because it was kept a secret from me. But I always felt out of place for several reasons. I looked different from the rest of the family. I was darker complexioned with dark brown hair. They were blond with gray-green eyes. One grandmother even had red hair. In my teen years, I became aware that it wasn't just my appearance that was different from my parents. My personality, my interests, my talents, my spirituality, were all very different from theirs and those differences were not particularly appreciated by them."

Suspecting the secret of one's adoption generates feelings of bewilderment, some adoptees report. Learning the truth pushes them to an entirely different level of emotion. It sends them into the wilderness.

"There are no easy steps to take in dealing with this crisis of the self," said Dr. Severson. "This crisis moves one into the desert of the soul . . . a wilderness of the heart. There will be changes. One will never be the same. How one comes out of the wilderness can't be predicted."

This journey is a walk into a wasteland, laid bare by silence and what feels like utter betrayal. It's a walk one begins alone. How one returns from the wandering has everything to do with time, process, support, understanding, and forgiveness.

Hope for Resolution

How does a person manage the past mismanagement of the most intimate detail of life—one's personal identity? How does a person regain a sense of self and stand on solid emotional and psychological ground? How does one face the people in life who often unknowingly and without harmful intent created the maze of secrets and maintained it at all costs?

For each adoptee who uncovers the reality of his adoption as an adult, the circumstances are different, the pain is unique. For some, still in the early stages of discovery, emotional balance and freedom from anguish feels completely out of reach. Others find themselves on a road leading out of the wilderness heading toward resolution and reconciliation.

The following stories portray real circumstances, real people, and real suffering. If you identify with them, their stories may give you guidance and hope.

Moya's Story

Moya Sealy Baker and her older brother grew up with a unique identity and heritage—that of American Indian. It was a heritage in which she was raised to respect and preserve its culture.

On a spring day in 1993, three months before her fifty-first birthday, Moya received an unsettling call from her fifty-two-year-old brother.

"Moya, are you sitting down?" he asked. "I have something to tell you." Jerry then began to explain that he had sent his birth certificate to the Chickasaw Nation Bureau of Indian Affairs to verify his Indian lineage in order to establish a small business minority status. A staff person found a problem and told him she could not verify that he was Indian because his birth certificate had been altered.

"Sir," she told Jerry, "either one or both of your parents' names have been changed or you are adopted. We can't verify your Indian ancestry."

Unable to reach Moya at work, Jerry called an aunt and asked her if she could verify his Indian heritage. Did she remember his birth? She told him she did not know much about his birth, but she remembered being told "when they adopted you and Moya, they told us you were Chickasaw and they didn't know about Moya." This confirmed what the Chickasaw Nation Bureau had said.

Shock engulfed Moya as her brother continued to relate his findings. "We are both adopted and we are not biological brother and sister."

The revelation of Moya's adoption happened on May 5, 1993. Jerry came to Oklahoma City and by 1:00 p.m. the afternoon of May 13, 1993, both Moya and her brother obtained a court order that would enable them to get a copy of their original birth certificates and adoption papers. By 4:30 they had found out who their mothers were—Jerry's was a Chickasaw Indian woman, father unknown. Moya's was her adopted mother's sister— a woman she had known all her life as her aunt. Her birth father was Hispanic. By 9:00 p.m. they were sixty-five miles away and in Jerry's birth mother's home. Moya's birth mother was traveling and it was the nineteenth of May before they could contact her.

"Both birth mothers," Moya related, "never wanted their secrets known. They had both married, both had four other children and had never told them. Both of their husbands had died and had never known their wives had given up a child."

Moya's harsh and jagged walk into the "desert" caused by the tightly held secret of her adoption was compounded by multiple tragedies.

Eleven years before the disclosure, Moya's delightful seven-month-old grandson drowned in a bathtub accident. Shortly after the sixth anniversary of Johnny's death, Charles, her only child and the one person she always felt connected to, committed suicide. He never recovered from the death of his son. Seven months later, her father died from a lengthy illness and eight months later, her mother died from a sudden illness. Two years later her husband's life was severely threatened with two heart attacks and life-saving bypass surgery. These tragic events sent her free falling into deep depression and despair. She was just resurfacing emotionally when the news of her adoptive status hit her.

"As an R.N. and a grief counselor, I'm aware of the issues that surface when death comes. I experienced them significantly with the death of my son, my grandson, and my parents. With their deaths, my future belief system was shattered. I didn't have anything left to link me to the future. I was left struggling with a major identity crisis, for I had been a daughter, a mother, a grandmother. My future was tied to these roles. With the deaths of my family, that future was gone," Moya anguished.

Continuing, she said, "When the news came that I was not who I thought myself to be, my whole past belief system shattered, too. I wasn't American Indian, not at all. My heritage was Mexican. I had no future—it had died. I had no true past—for it had all been a lie."

It has been two years since the unveiling of the secret. Where does Moya find herself in the process toward emotional, physical, and spiritual healing?

"I struggle every day. I have to work really hard at just being here," she said. "I am not so angry at the decision that was made fifty years ago as I am that as times changed we were not told and never would have been told. This is what has devastated me today. I'm angry at the lies and the betrayal and the fact that I now cannot get answers from those who could have told me. I struggle with the bitterness because this was all so preventable."

Although Moya's wounds are fresh—the pain a part of everyday life—she is able to extend to others words of advice:

"The first thing you should do if this happens to you is seek the support of those who have walked a similar road. My husband, of course, supports me, but my brother, even living in Florida, was a tremendous help, for he understood what it felt like. Second, find a group that deals with adoption, loss, grief, some group that can help you through the recovery process and get professional counseling.

"I've lost a part of myself. I'm trying desperately to find out who I really am."

Karen's Story

In the summer of 1990, Karen Slagle, age thirty-two, and her family made plans to attend a family reunion in Arkansas. She had no idea the visit would alter the course of her life and relationships forever. The experience was so traumatic that in order to put the pieces together, Karen reconstructed a journal of the events of the week that shoved her into a wilderness of personhood.

Remembering June 16, 1990

I went to the family reunion in Arkansas. As I was looking about at all my relatives, I noticed how much the family resembled one another. Steve (my husband) made the comment, "You are the prettiest one here; you don't look like the rest of the family."

I wanted to come to this reunion for two reasons. First, I did it for my dad, and second I was extremely interested in tracing my roots. I had found out about an Indian Chief, Red Eagle, who was an ally of Andrew Jackson in the 1820s. That was of great interest to me. I went around asking questions of all the older people at the reunion. I looked at pictures and found some of my father when he was a little boy. I studied his face intently trying to find some resemblance in me or my children. I had always wondered why I was so different from everyone in my family.

At the end of the day an older cousin came up to Steve and me. His wife said, "Oh, I remember you when you were just a little bitty thing right after Clyde and Betty *got you*."

When they walked away, I said to Steve, "Did you notice anything strange in that conversation?" He replied, "Yeah, got you from where? Under a rock or what?"

That evening, at my mother's home, I pored through the pictures with intense persistence looking for anything that might give me the truth without asking Mom. I was fearful of asking her. I have had too many negative confrontations with her in my life and wanted to avoid a scene.

I spent five hours looking at a chicken crate *full* of pictures of me growing up. One of the last pictures I looked at caught my attention. It was a picture of Mom holding me when I was one week old. She was in a form-fitting dress and was shapely. I really knew at that point that I was adopted, but I needed it confirmed.

Remembering June 17, 1990

The next morning, Father's Day, I couldn't stand not knowing for sure. I went back to Mother's house and went into her bedroom. I told her what my cousin had said. I then asked her, "Mom, am I adopted too?" She said no too quickly. I replied to her, "Mom, if I am, please tell me. You are my mother and always will be, but I have the right to know." She still denied it.

Knowing the truth, I pulled out the picture I had found the night before. I said to her, "I'm sorry to hurt you like this, but in this

111

picture of you and me you look too good. I've had two babies and I know this is not a picture of a woman who recently gave birth to a baby." She began to cry and then said, "You were adopted at birth."

She told me that as long as I didn't know, I was *hers*. She said things would never be the same between us again. I tried to reassure her, but it was no use. She dismissed me saying, "Now you'll go and find you have a pretty mother and you won't love me anymore." I was hurt, shocked, and angry.

We left for home. I cried all the way. I felt betrayed, crushed, devastated, confused, hurt, and stupid all rolled up into one. It was a horrible day. I cried myself to sleep that night. Steve was very supportive and felt badly because he could not cheer me up as usual. Just as I got to sleep, Steve shook me and shouted with excitement. "Brian's not going to be bald." (My father has been bald since he was twenty years old.) Leave it to my dear Steve to brighten up *any* dark situation. That was the only laugh I had that day.

Remembering June 18, 1990

When I woke up, I was driven to search for the truth. I felt desperate for knowledge. The rug had been pulled out from my neat and tidy little idea of who I am. I called the Department of Vital Statistics to find out how I could get a copy of my original birth certificate. The man told me to "just go down to the courthouse and get a court order. We will release them to you."

Remembering June 19, 1990

My best friend, Anita, went with me to see the judge. I was not prepared for the question of why I wanted to know. My request was denied without medical reason.

That evening I called my aunt thinking my mother's sister might know something. All she knew from family gossip was that my birth mother had been married at the time of my birth with several children already. That certainly didn't make me feel any better. I thought if she was married with children already, then what was wrong with me? I felt rejected and unwanted.

For Karen, the day she found out about her adoption and the confusion of the weeks that followed is branded into her memory. As time progressed, the revelation resulted in serious trauma that sparked both emotional and physical upheaval.

"After the secret came out, I became physically ill," Karen related. "I developed hypoglycemia and gastrointestinal problems. I became extremely tired—incredibly fatigued. It was not just the revelation of 'being adopted' that triggered the emotional and physical stresses. It was a blessing to finally have my questions answered. It explained so much about who I am, why I have certain personality traits and physical characteristics.

"What triggered the problems I am experiencing is the betrayal of trust," Karen said. "Adoption was not a new term to me. I have a sister, Margie, whom they adopted when I was fourteen. It was because of me that she has learned of her adoption. I told my mom when she was born that we had to tell her. It was her right to know. How ironic!"

Following the revelation of Karen's adoption, Karen took steps to deal with her trauma. "What I did right away was a flurry of activity. I searched for my birth mother and found her. My adoptive mother rejected me because of the search. After an eighteen-month growing relationship with my birth mother, the revelation of another sister and my search for her ended our communication. I have been rejected by both of my mothers. I struggle with feelings of being detached and unloved.

"I advise anyone in the same situation to seek support right away from someone who has been in similar circumstances. First, I started helping others in their searches. Looking back, I think all that activity was an effort to deny or avoid my own pain. I thought I was coping by helping others, but again I was pushing aside my own needs. I would advise others in this situation to get into counseling right away. Adoption support groups are a great place to begin."

Tammy's Story

On April 27, 1991, Tammy Pasela received a call from her sister, Lisa, who was noticeably upset. Tammy immediately thought that because her mother was critically ill the worst had happened. But that was not the reason for the call. It was something almost as traumatic.

"Tammy," Lisa said. "All day today, Mom has been calling out for us . . . she has been calling out for her adopted daughters. I really didn't think much of it until tonight when I happened to mention it to our aunt. You won't believe what she said. She asked, 'You mean you girls don't know?'"

Tammy, stunned by the news, told her sister she would handle this. "I will call Dad," Tammy reassured her. "He'll tell us the truth."

Immediately Tammy dialed her father's number. He was at his farmhouse in southern Ohio hunting. Tammy's parents were divorced and both had remarried. When he picked up the phone Tammy said, "Dad, I have a question for you. Are we adopted?"

There was total silence on the other end and Tammy repeated the question. All her father kept saying was "I love you." Soon he began to cry. He rarely did this. All he could say was, "I love you."

Tammy repeated her question again, already knowing in her heart the truth. She felt the need to comfort her father, assuring him that no matter what, they would be okay. He finally told her that both girls had been adopted, Lisa in 1957 and Tammy in 1959.

Tammy's mother lived just two short weeks following the revelation. Tammy was only able to talk to her one last time.

"I had to tell her I loved her anyway," Tammy commented. "But that wasn't enough to get her to talk to us about it. She didn't respond."

After her mother's death, Tammy learned that had her mother never uttered those words, the truth would have surfaced at the reading of her will. The girls were referred to as "adopted daughters." What followed for Tammy was incredible emotional trauma.

Tammy realized early in the experience that she could not bear the pain alone. The first thing she did was contact an adoption support group in her area. The group helped her not only to deal with the emotional and psychological injury, but to take practical steps in locating birth family information.

"I knew I needed help to handle this. I felt like I was losing my mind. All I had established my life upon had been ripped from me," Tammy declared. "All of a sudden I had no true heritage, no medical history, nothing.

"One of the most helpful things I did in counseling," Tammy said, "was to talk. I mean talk and talk and talk. I talked about my family, my anger, my fears, everything. I talked until it was all out."

A year after the secret was disclosed, Tammy made a decision to locate her birth mother, which she did on June 8, 1992. The reunion has been positive and exciting for her.

"I've been blessed in finding my birth mother and three half-siblings. Even though they live quite a distance way, I've spent time with all of them."

Over time, how has Tammy processed this traumatic, life-jarring event?

"I have periods of anger still today," she offered. "But I'm an optimistic person and a survivor. I determined that I would not get stuck in anger. Sometimes I want to cry out, 'If you could have trusted me enough to love you, this wouldn't have happened.' I can't get into the blame game or make judgments. After all, I haven't done too badly in my life. I realize but for the grace of God, there go I."

Alissa's Story

"I guess I should have caught on a lot earlier," Alissa said of her adoptive status. "But I didn't. I must have blocked out all the cues."

Alissa's adoptive circumstances vary somewhat from that of most adoptees. Alissa was raised by her biological mother and the man she thought to be her biological father. Quite by accident, one rainy afternoon four years ago, an aunt let the secret slip.

"We were sitting in her living room discussing the situation of a little neighborhood youngster. She was being raised by a relative with no contact from her birth father at all.

"'I wonder,' my aunt asked me, 'if Becky will question anyone about her birth father? By the way, why haven't you ever pursued it?'

"My mind went blank with her question—it stunned me so. I stammered a minute, asking what she meant and pretending I just didn't understand what she was saying. I was in shock. All I could do was mumble some excuse and leave. I had to ask someone who knew—my mother."

After hearing from her mother that the man who raised her was not her biological father but her adoptive father, Alissa still had great difficulty processing the news. As she began to mull the whole thing over in her mind, she recalled situations and comments along the way that should have given her a clue there was something different about her.

"I felt like one of those little dinghies tied behind the big boat," Alissa related. "Suddenly the dingy is cut loose to drift out to sea. Waves of fear, loneliness, and anger washed over me, depending on the day and the time. Mostly, a feeling of extreme isolation engulfed me. Suddenly I felt I didn't belong anymore. I wasn't fully a part of any family."

As time progressed, Alissa's feelings, especially that of anger, deepened.

"My anger was not so much with my birth father, whom I met two months after the secret came out. He acknowledged he had been wrong. My anger was with my mother and other family members who held on so tightly to the silence. The hurt I felt because of the broken trust was far more intense than the fact that my birth father abandoned me," Alissa stated.

"Sometimes it felt like a dream—like this could not have really happened. I've talked with my birth father on several occasions, but my family—my mother, my brother, and sister haven't allowed me to discuss this since the initial conversation. I feel like I have to pretend it didn't happen.

My pain has not been acknowledged. My mother has never said she is sorry, and I guess that's what I really want to hear."

As Alissa realized she was walking deep into a wilderness, walled off by anger and bitterness, she knew she had come to a significant crossroad. She could choose to stay angry and bitter or turn and walk out of that dark, desolate place onto a road that would lead to healing and inner resolution.

"I decided when things broke loose and I felt so intensely angry that I would not, I could not, stay in that emotional whirlpool. I would move past it. Having made that choice, I've tried to extend forgiveness—not so much for their sake, but for mine. God showed me that forgiveness is not just getting rid of angry feelings; it's accepting that they owe me nothing. I can't sit and wait for lost days to be made up and keep track of 'nice' gestures. I will not keep score.

"I've also been able to find meaning in all of this. I have a better understanding of people because of the trauma and depression I experienced. I have a better understanding of myself, because I know I've learned much. I also have a deeper relationship with God because He enabled me to extend forgiveness—it was not of myself."

CLOSING THE WOUND

According to Dr. Severson, finding out one's adoptive status as an adult strikes intensely and deeply at one's sense of reality. What develops for the adult adoptee afterward is determined by several factors. All play a significant role in the heart and mind of the adopted person as she goes about the business of redefining who she is.

First, where that person is in her life span is a critical factor in regaining balance, Dr. Severson feels. Is the person married? Does he or she have children? maybe even grandchildren? Another consideration is the age of the birth parents should a reunion be pursued.

A second factor in regaining equilibrium has a lot to do with one's personality type, Dr. Severson commented. "If the adopted person is an understanding person, he will deal with the issue and go on. If his personality is highly sensitive, or he is emotionally vulnerable, his world may turn upside down. A person doesn't have to become impaired by this revelation. He may have trouble committing to other relationships or trouble trusting people in general, but it can be worked through."

In any transgression there comes a time when we must decide what to do with the anger, resentment, and bitterness that consumes us. To consider forgiveness can seem almost inconceivable. Don't we have a right to consider some offenses unforgivable?

As much as we may deny it, a lack of forgiveness may signal that "something more is going on besides our rightful and understandable refusal to forget what has been done to us."[6] There are several reasons why an adopted adult may actively or unknowingly avoid forgiveness.

Why We Choose Not to Forgive

We may choose not to forgive our parents for the secret they kept from us because our unforgiveness can be used "to punish them." Conspicuous absence at special family gatherings, avoiding phone calls, "forgetting" special occasions, all are passive ways to pay back our parents for the "crime" they committed.

We may choose not to forgive our parents because by "denying forgiveness, we allow ourselves to feel power over them," a power that was originally denied us.

We have been victims of lies, deceptions, and even reality. Once the secret is out, we may sense a feeling of power over those who previously owned it.

We may choose not to forgive our parents because it may seem like we condone what they did—it will let them off the hook.

We can choose to stay angry and distant due to the incredible sense of betrayal. Doing so assures us the walls will stay up; the distance will be maintained. We can continue to inflict pain on our adoptive parents as a long-term, ongoing reminder of their wrongdoing.

We may choose not to forgive our parents because forgiveness is difficult work. It requires us to walk on a road paved by uncertainty and to face personal issues of our own honesty and intimacy—all without any guarantee of mutual receptivity.

Extending an open hand of forgiveness places us in an extremely vulnerable situation. Seemingly irreparable damage may have been done through word and actions motivated by hurt and betrayal. Our work then becomes to evaluate if taking the risk by admitting our own wrongdoing is worth it.

Dwayne's Story

While preparing for a trip overseas, Dwayne West attempted to get his birth certificate. Weeks of confusion and misinformation created a suspicion that something just wasn't right. Late on a Sunday afternoon, Dwayne went to his parents' home. He had to ask them a question: Was he adopted?

That afternoon, after moments of silence, his father confirmed

Dwayne's suspicions. They had chosen not to tell him; they thought it was best, and they were told it was best.

Dwayne's anger and rage at the betrayal sent him out of the house with promises of permanent severance of their relationship.

For weeks Dwayne refused their phone calls and avoided seeing them in familiar places determined to find a balance to the chaos that raged within him. Finally, at the advice of a friend who had listened to his pain, Dwayne decided to call his parents. He was tired of being stuck in such a destructive emotional storm.

"I didn't want to call them that evening, but I could no longer live like this. Yes, they had betrayed me. Yes, I could not think of anything worse one person could do to another. But yes, they had also loved me and I them.

"When Dad answered the phone, after the silence, I could hear the deep sorrow in his voice. I could hear my mother's plea for forgiveness through strained words and muffled tears. My father told me he had no idea a choice they made so many years ago might cost him the love of his only son.

"I chose at that moment to say, 'I forgive you.' I chose at that moment to close the wound. Instead of staying separated by walls of anger and unforgiveness, we are now free to talk about what happened to us and to begin rebuilding a relationship ripped apart by a decision made in ignorance."

Other Stories of Forgiveness
Other adults who have made this difficult journey through forgiveness have discovered powerful, healing principles. Dwight Wolter's viewpoint is valid here:

> Walking around angry at my parents squanders my precious energy, confuses my emotions, and depletes my physical health.
>
> To forgive is to clear a space for change to occur. Plants need to be pruned so that light can filter through the remaining leaves and reach the soil where new life is struggling to grow. *The secret* is like those dead leaves. I can keep watering and watering them, but they will not spring to life.
>
> Forgiveness does not happen by reading a book or by doing any one thing. Any wound, any rip in the fabric of a relationship takes time to heal. And it takes work. Festering wounds need to be opened and drained, cleaned out and exposed to fresh air and light. I've learned to accept that the journey toward forgiveness begins in

pain. And I've been able to see that these uncomfortable feelings do not last forever. Time—and work—can heal this wound.[7]

◆ ◆ ◆

I am not sure that the goal of modern therapy is forgiveness or reconciliation. Instead, therapy often helps us to justify our anger. That's unfortunate, because we must get beyond our anger if we are to experience the depth and fullness of life in relationship with others. A part of taking care of myself is the work of reconciliation—forgiving those who have wounded me. And I can't do that in the privacy of a therapist's office or by reading a book or by wishing things were better. Reconciliation cannot happen in a vacuum. It can only happen in the encounter between two people. Therapy is usually aimed at the health of the individual, but it sometimes fails to take into account that we must live in healthy communities, healthy relationships, to be happy and at peace.
—Jan Campbell, age 45

The best advice I can give an adult who has just found out he or she is adopted is, allow yourself time. Take time to let this new status settle in, to process what it means in your life, to adjust to this new "identity." Now is not the time to make potentially life-altering decisions. Until you've lived with this new information for a while, don't rush into a search or cut off the people who deceived you. Deal with one thing at a time. Searching immediately will not heal your open wounds; it may complicate an already overwhelming situation.
—Betsie Norris, age 34

CHAPTER EIGHT

WHEN THE PIECES DON'T FIT: FINDING DEAD ENDS OR DEATH

❖

For almost four years, I've written and called and sleuthed for shreds of information, tiny clues that would lead me a little closer to information about my birth family. Sometimes one little fact—like a date or something someone thought she remembered—would lead to months of searching. I ran into so many roadblocks. Some people were compassionate; a few stretched the rules to help me. Many people told me to mind my own business, not to go where I might not be wanted, not to make trouble. But still I kept trying, believing in my heart that knowing something or someone is always better than not knowing.

KATIE LEE CRANE, AGE 47

The journey began with hope. For some the hope was to find answers to questions that had plagued them a lifetime. For others, it was a hope to touch the face and hold the hand of the one person who was more intimately connected to them than any other person on the face of the earth.

Yet for these, their search did not lead to hope fulfilled; it led to hope deferred. It began with trembling anticipation. It drew to a close in the midst of confusion, frustration, disappointment, loss, and pain. It was a journey that would call for a restructuring of their hopes and dreams and a reordering of the needs of the heart. For some it has ended unexpectedly— with hope redefined.

From the ranks of thousands of adult adoptees involved in the search for birth family members comes a number who find heartbreaking disappointment. For some adopted persons, the search stretches from months into years with nothing but brick walls at every turn. For others a search effort filled with passion and anticipation crumbles at the discovery of the death of their birth parents.

How do you deal with unending, seemingly unanswerable questions? How do you encounter the reality of the death of a birth parent and move on with a sense of closure and peace? What do you do when the pieces won't fit? These dilemmas need solutions that lead to resolution and recovery. "Hope deferred makes the heart sick," but hope redefined moves us toward wellness and wholeness.

FACING DEAD ENDS

"I have known people whose searches have gone on for fifteen to twenty years," reported Kate Burke of the American Adoption Congress.[1] These dead ends exist for a variety of reasons, from sealed, destroyed, or altered records to self-imposed roadblocks. Listening to the experiences of adopted persons who have experienced dead ends can comfort you if your own pieces don't fit.

Paula's Story
As a teenager, Paula Griffis-Walton Pedigo, now forty-one, discovered a secret that altered the course of her life and sent her on a journey to find someone who could tell her the rest of the story. The many pieces that came together should have finished the puzzle, but they haven't.

1971
Paula finds out about her adoption. A senior in high school with too much time on her hands before her mom and dad get home from work—Paula

figures out how to get into the family safe. One envelope with Daddy's handwriting says "Paula Ann's Adoption." She had never heard the term, so obviously she opens and reads the contents. It was the first time she sees her birth mother's name on her original birth certificate. What a shock! She reads further—Father: unknown . . . even more of a shock. About three months later she finally asked her parents, "What does adopted mean?" Her father said nothing. Her mother was enraged and said, "You're better off, don't ask again!" Paula struggles with a conflictive relationship with her mother. Time goes on and Paula makes up stories in her mind about her birth mother.

1976
March 17. Paula's father dies after fighting cancer for five years. He is only fifty-six. This is devastating to her as they were always close. He was always so kind and gentle, unlike the harsh treatment Paula received from her mother. He never mentioned the adoption.

Paula continues to struggle with her mother's nonacceptance.

1984
Paula is now married with a husband and two children. She visits an aunt in Houston, her mother's sister. She freely tells Paula a "few" things about her adoption, her birth mother, her birth sister, and her adoptive parents. Paula learns for the first time that her birth mother and sister lived with her adoptive parents prior to her birth. It is also the first time she knew she had a sister.

1984-92
Relationship with adoptive mother has deteriorated to nonexistent.

1992
June. Paula receives a call from her aunt, "Your mother is dying, it's time for *you* to make up to her." Paula and her family go to the hospital against Paula's better judgment. She wonders, "Why should I go? She rejected us." Her mother doesn't recognize them for a long time. But then she improves and is discharged from the hospital. The next ten months Paula sees her once a week.

1993
March 5. Another call comes. Her mother probably won't live through the weekend. Paula is told she must make some decisions. Her mother improves slightly and goes home.

March 21. She worsens again but survives until April 1.

April 3. The day of the funeral, Paula's cousin, her aunt's son, gives Paula her adoption papers, but the original birth certificate is missing. Paula is the only child of her adoptive parents, but their estate is left to this cousin to do with as he pleases. Paula can't afford to fight it. She cries out, "I want my birth mother more than ever now."

Although Paula searched occasionally before, she had never felt the intensity that engulfed her following the death of her adoptive mother.

"It is with great passion I have begun this search again. The passion comes from the support of some of my mother's sisters and my husband. Cousins my age and younger knew all along that I was adopted. Everyone thought I knew too! I think of my father often. How could he take this to the grave with him? Why did he? *Why? Why? Why?*"

When beginning her search this time, Paula did so in a more thorough way. "I had explored my adoption on and off for twenty years, but never kept records of anything. When I started again last year, after Mother died, it was from scratch trying to use my original papers and interviewing family members. I have files and files of records now just from the last eighteen months. Correspondence logs, conversation logs, charts and graphs. I have read every book out there, made literally hundreds of phone calls, written dozens and dozens of letters to everyone, but with absolutely no success."

What has been the result for Paula? Dead ends and empty hopes. "I feel I've come so close, then other times I feel like I'm so far off track. I believe it's on purpose because my adoptive mother wanted it that way. Things are so hidden, lied about, names changed, information lost. There's no end to the trail of disguise and inaccuracy."

Paula's search and the dead ends that plague her have left her with unresolved issues and unsettled feelings. "I haven't put them to rest and I probably won't until I can find the answers. I feel like I'm the victim, but why? What have I done to deserve this?

"If my birth family doesn't want me, okay. I'd be disappointed, but no more so than with all the dead ends. I'd like to know about them . . . my birth family. Was I really better off? Do they know about me?

"My feelings are mixed with disappointment, hope, hate, love, and bitterness. I would really like to have a family . . . I'm an only child with two deceased parents, but I have two children and a husband who are loving and supportive and go through my feelings with me every day."

Paula's dead ends are a result of what appears to be intended secrecy. For another adoptee, the dead ends are a result of the barred doors of closed records and agency limitations.

Bruce's Story

Bruce Helwig, a thirty-four-year-old adopted person, has been in and out of his search for a number of years. A writer, Bruce recorded his intense feelings about a dead-end return to the adoption agency. In the process he gives voice to the heart and soul of a searcher stepping into what feels like a dark, unknown place.

Across the street was my birth place, in a manner of speaking. It was an unusually pleasant midsummer day in New York City. I'd taken a bus from the Village to the Upper East Side, the address scribbled on a scrap of paper. Nearly shaking with fear as I stood across from the building, I took comfort in the belief that this moment was at once chosen and fated. I could approach the entrance. I might even enter and speak. If I just lingered in front, wearing an impassive mask to hide my panic, everything would be okay.

I hesitated just a moment before opening the glass outer door. Before she even spoke, the receptionist recognized me. Not personally, but as a type. She made the stock "may-I-help-you-sir" phrase sound heartfelt.

"Some thirty years ago I was adopted from this place; my sister, too." I wanted to say more, but my tongue went thick. Mercifully, the receptionist asked an easy question. "What was your name?" In a flash I realized I was being treated according to a therapeutic model. It was comforting. The agency had learned that people like me might arrive on their doorstep at any time and at any age. They had decided we were fragile, needy, and anxious for support, and they were right. A lost little boy looking for my parents, I gave the nice lady my name and felt sheepish relief when she gestured to the waiting room.

A few moments later, a large handsome woman in her early forties stepped quietly to my side. She confirmed my name (who else could I be?) and motioned for me to follow her. She said she would go back upstairs and pull my file, but I knew she'd just done so, and had already had a quick look at what it contained. I sat down to wait for her return, glancing at two double doors with an emergency exit sign above them. Memories came.

The last time I'd been here was 1964. We'd come in from Westchester—my father, mother, sister, and I—to sign papers making my sister official. I've always recalled it as "the day we got Janice," though she'd been living with us for close to a year by then.

Much later I realized that, in this adopted child's mind, she did not become "real" until we kept that appointment. Janice was a toddler; I was four.

The trip back to the agency was an essential though unplanned step toward self-empowerment. I needed to claim their space, however fearfully, and add my voice to the chorus of agency adoptees who believe that open records are the only humane choice. We have been legally divorced from our evidence of birth. A right every other citizen takes for granted is denied by state and local authorities. It is no accident of fate, but a policy decreed by "naturally parented" people who cannot possibly comprehend our need to know.

When the woman returned, she asked me humanely, "Where are you in your search?"

I answered, "As I'm sure you know from my file, I contacted the agency about eighteen months ago seeking nonidentifying information. It's taken me the year since I received a reply to process it and get this far. I happened to be in New York and have a lot of questions about what I was sent."

"What kinds of questions do you have?" was her ambiguous reply. We were on very shaky and highly subjective ground and I couldn't tell whether this was merely rhetorical or an invitation to ask away.

"For example, about my birth father. The letter provided some data on ethnicity and employment, but nothing about his family." The woman was not forthcoming. "I'm really not familiar with your case," she said. "The records have been returned to storage since you wrote and the caseworker assigned is no longer with us." I'd met the management. Innocently phrased probes weren't going to get me anywhere.

A confrontational tact seemed appropriate. "There are also discrepancies between what my parents remember and what the letter suggested," I stated coldly. "How can I confirm, or at least reconcile that with what was provided? I want to know everything you can possibly tell me. I also want to see any relevant documents that are not legally sealed."

She asked how long I would be in New York. For adoptees outside the area, she explained, letters were the most effective means of communication. In that case, I was ready to start writing. "May I have a paper and a pen, please? I'd like to leave a written request with you before I go."

For the next half-hour I composed a formal letter with detailed requests for clarification and follow-up questions. It was polite and well reasoned, but restated my desire to have any and all nonidentifying information in the agency's possession. When the woman returned I asked for a photocopy and she obliged. Then I left through the glass doors with the assurance that I would be contacted by a caseworker.

The agency sent me a brush-off letter months after my visit, attributing their inaction to a shortage of caseworkers and requesting that I later remind them of my request. Preposterous, yet instructive. My next visit to the atypical birthplace I share with my sister must be negotiated. An adoptee from this agency may arrive unannounced once or twice in his or her life, but no more.[2]

Secrecy and agency limitations imposed by the state law are just two of the seemingly insurmountable barriers creating a dead-end search. A third is caused not by something without, but within.

Joanne's Story

When Joanne put the receiver back on the phone, she wondered to herself, *Will I get any closer this time . . . and follow through?*

Joanne Dummond had been searching for her birth mother for nearly twelve years. At least, the search organization helping her had. Every once in a while the search group would call, excited with a possible lead. Their only request was that Joanne follow through with it. However, something within her stopped. She couldn't follow through.

"Some people put up self-imposed dead ends," related Kate Burke. "They put up their own roadblocks. They say they've been searching for years but have not done the work on their own search. They want to leave the process to others. It seems they are incapable of doing anything for themselves when it comes to taking the final steps toward finding a birth parent."

Reasons for the blockage for many searchers stifled by self-imposed roadblocks can range from fear of rejection to fear of acceptance and closeness. They may fear they can't handle what they might find, such as mental illness or poverty.

Never getting past roadblocks for some adoptees brings them to a decision-making point in the road. When does a searcher know to give up? Kate Burke suggests two guidelines:

1. *When Obsession Is the Rule Instead of the Exception*

There does come a time when an adopted person has to give up. A sign that it's time, according to Kate, is when the search has consumed the adoptee for a long period of time; when it has become such an obsession over the months, even years, that everything else in the searcher's life has been shelved.

2. *When the Search Is Emotionally Self-Abusive*

Finding oneself in the midst of a search places the adoptee on an emotional roller coaster. When information is found—exhilaration. When information is wrong—disappointment. When a sealed record is opened—anticipation. When information is incomplete—discouragement. "When the adoptee has spent too much time living on the edge of the search, it can become emotionally abusive," Kate said. "There comes a time when he must make a decision to lay the search aside." When the pain created by unending barriers drains one's ability to live fully and completely, it may be time to redefine the hope. How can that be done?

"Finding dead ends is very hard. If a searcher cannot find a person, he can perhaps find places," advises Dr. Joyce Maguire Pavao. "He can go to the places, explore his heritage. He can perhaps find people who knew his birth parents. It doesn't totally take away the sense of loss in not locating birth parents, but the process itself can be revealing and helpful."[3]

Encountering dead ends in the search process requires the adoptee to step back and reorganize his hopes—his dreams. Finding a different "unexpected" also calls for the reordering of one's world.

Death of a Dream

Hearing the disappointing words, "Your birth mother (or father) has died," evokes incredible sorrow and bitter disappointment for many adoptees who intellectually knew of the possibility but blocked it from the heart. To emotionally survive such a momentous disappointment compels one to rewrite the script. Those who have walked that path can best speak of their pain. Some are still enveloped by feelings of defeat and grief. With time and process, others have worked through the anguish to redefine their dreams, to redefine their hope.

All the Signs Told Us She Was Alive

"Although I realized my search could end at the grave, I discarded that thought as quickly as an expectant woman discards the thought of stillbirth."

Patti Jo Burtnett, age twenty-seven, made the decision to search when she was a teenager. She postponed an active effort until her early twenties.

"I joined a search group when I was twenty-four years old," Patti Jo said. "My hopes soared when I met other people who had successful, happy, joyous reunions. It was then I decided I would devote every effort toward my own search."

Over the following months, Patti Jo, with the help of Adoption Network Cleveland support group, found encouraging signs. She obtained her mother's original birth certificate, which enabled her to trace her mother through other sources.

"Everything kept coming up as current. My birth mother had a valid driver's license and other reports were up to date. We finally went back to her last known address, thinking she may have recently moved. The current landlady had no knowledge of her. Past receipts of just a few years ago also showed no evidence of her ever living there. At that point, I was really confused."

The next step Patti Jo took was to check death records. Perhaps her mother had recently died. "We went to the public library and searched back two years and found nothing. Then we asked the librarian to check back further. Just a few days later, in September 1992, the horrible call came. They had found the information. My birth mother had died at age thirty-six in 1976. She had died of mysterious causes. There was no body, she had been cremated and buried."

Patti Jo reacted to the harsh news as understandably unsettling. "Throughout the search, all the clues pointed to a live person, so discovering her death was extremely jarring. I went into a cycle of emotions—sadness, pain, grief, and anger. The anger comes, I think, from having such high expectations and hopes and not being realistically prepared for what I found."

What steps has Patti Jo taken in working with her shattered desires? After finding the death of her birth mother, Patti Jo and her husband went to the cemetery. It was the only thing she knew to do.

"Going to the grave was the closest I'll ever get to my mother. On that day, my husband and I walked through rows of gravestones looking for hers. He found it. It felt very weird to walk over to it and see her name on the stone. It made me realize the finality of it all. This is as far as I'm going to get. I sat down and cried. Even today, I'm still angry at the loss. I had no choice. I had no chance."

My Expectations Were Too High

Erika Zappa, age twenty-eight, started her search after completing a college research project on opening adoption records. She had no clue that the seemingly innocent search would impact her life so deeply.

After Erika actively began to search, she formed a picture in her mind of what her reunion would be like.

"When I was about a week away from getting the information about my birth mother, I remember thinking, *A week from now and she and I will be together.* I thought we probably looked exactly alike, based on the non-identifying information. I expected we'd have the same likes and dislikes, the same talents and viewpoints.

"I will never forget the afternoon in the late summer of 1992 when the search consultant helping me called. 'I don't have good news for you. Your birth mother died several years ago. It was an apparent accidental death and she died of cardiac arrest. She was only forty-one.'"

The emotional downhill ride Erika experienced sent her into a whirlpool of feelings.

> At first I experienced terrible sadness, disbelief, and then anger. It was very painful and emotional. I cried for a whole day, driving in the car, sitting at home. I would just cry. I couldn't talk about it because I would start crying all over again. I had always thought this would be the greatest experience of my life. I thought we'd bond and be inseparable. I thought I would meet the one person on earth who truly loved me.
>
> Now, knowing I will never, ever meet her, see her, touch her, talk to her ever in my entire life angers me. It is incomprehensible. I just wanted to talk to her, to ask her why she gave me up and if she thought about me on my birthday. I'll never be able to do that. There will always be a part of me missing. I just hope we can be together in eternity.

Although Erika never met her birth mother, she did meet her birth grandmother. Her grandmother told her of her birth mother's lifelong grief following her relinquishment decision. "My grandmother told me she believed my birth mother really died of a broken heart. She never got over giving me up. Every birthday she became extremely depressed and sad.

"What else was interesting is that my grandmother gave me a video Mother had made six months before her death. It was a uniquely relevant video. She was going through her house describing those things that were important to her and her feelings attached to those things. I haven't been able to watch the video all the way through yet. It's too painful."

Although Erika continues to feel an incredible emotional gap because of the unexpected premature death of her birth mother, she took one more step toward resolution and that was to visit the grave.

"I went to her grave for the first time in April 1994, on the ninth anniversary of her death. I went feeling that I would handle it pretty well. Being overwhelmed with emotion and crying was not what I expected myself to do, but that's what happened. I just stood there and wept and kept saying to myself, 'Here she is and this is as close as I will EVER be.'"

MOVING TOWARD RESOLUTION

If your search has ended at the grave of a birth parent, how can you resolve the losses around such finality? How can you walk through this valley of the shadow and emerge reconciled and at peace? Is it possible?

"When I meet with an adoptee who has found death at the end of his or her search, what I hear initially is a deep sigh—'Oh well' uttered with incredible sadness," says Kate Burke. "Then they begin the long, difficult process of grieving. It's a complex process because they are grieving an abstract—someone they have no memory of seeing or touching."

In her book, *Journey of the Adopted Self*, Betty Jean Lifton comments:

It is a difficult process, for this is not the recognized loss of a mother that brings sympathy and comfort from family and friends. Even those who have seen their mother only a few times are over-whelmed by the impact of their grief. This dead mother was the woman who gave you life. Your body, born from hers, feels wrenched by its disintegration. . . . I did not hear of my mother's death until four months after it occurred. It was the end of a dark fairytale in which we could not rescue each other or ourselves. She took her grief and her loss and her secrets with her, just as she took some part of that child she had held onto and who continues to hold onto her.[4]

Katie Lee Crane, undaunted by years of dead ends and roadblocks

131

eventually found that her birth mother had died. Her walk toward resolution began at that discovery and in many ways continues today.

The years of searching were intense. I had volunteer and paid searchers from five states working with me to find my birth mother. Twice I found the wrong person. Each time I was devastated. The second time I was so distraught I created a *funeral for a fantasy*. Sitting at my dining table, candles surrounding a bouquet of daffodils, I wept as I officially *buried* my fantasy. The person I'd come to know from conversations with searchers and neighbors—the one who was a nurse, who had brown hair and brown eyes, the one who'd lived on Olive Street, who was intelligent, strong-willed, sweet and likable—*that person was not my birth mother*.

Only two weeks before a scheduled trip to Cleveland did I discover a clue that suggested my search might end there. Those two weeks were cloak-and-dagger weeks, with a friend literally calling me en route with new pieces of information.

On my second day in Cleveland, I went to city hall and requested the death certificate of a woman who might be my birth mother. She was. She had died of a blood clot in 1968 at the age of forty-six. I was to turn forty-six in twenty-two days.

The death certificate told me where she had lived, where she had died, and where she was buried. Before I left the city I visited all three places. When I went to her grave, I took one long-stemmed red rose and placed it there. I stayed by the marker, swimming in mud from an early spring snow, and spoke these words to her.

My hands are raw. My tears are crusting on my cheeks. My feet and ankles and gloves are covered with mud—so is your grave.

LOIS K. SMITH
WIFE, MOTHER
1921-1968

I brought you a rose. It's a symbol of the blood that killed you, the blood that gave me life, and thorns that hurt us both. You gave me life. The search gave me my self and my mother and the words: "You didn't make a mistake!"

Goodbye, Lois. Hello. Rest in peace.

Now I must surrender the fantasies—bury them all today—and hold up the complex and ambiguous and painful truth: You are gone and I never knew you. I never got to love you. But I will, from this day forward, honor your memory and praise God for the life you gave me.

Blessed be. Amen.

On the long trip home in the car, I cried as if my mother had just died. She had, for me. On that trip I decided I wanted to do something on my forty-sixth birthday to celebrate my life. I did not want to spend my forty-seventh year expecting to die just because she died in hers. I planned a naming/dedication (like a baptism) in which I took back the name Lee which had been given me at birth. It was my way of giving birth to Lee all over again, only not alone and in shame this time, but surrounded by loving friends and in great joy—the way every baby deserves to be born. It was a joyful occasion in which I gave thanks for the gifts from all four of my parents, the two I knew and the two I never knew, recognizing how each in their own way, shaped me and my life.

The search is complete, but the process is never over.[5]

A Word on International Searches

For those adopted internationally, the hope of ever reconnecting to birth family members is dim. Some begin with no hope, for some hope is ignited, for most hope is redefined. Often abandoned as infants in public places like police stations or left at orphanages due to the harsh economic, social, or political conditions within their home country, international adoptees generally grow up with the knowledge that what little information they have is all that will ever be possible to obtain. This was the case for one Korean adoptee.

Susan Soon Keum Cox, director of development for Holt International Children's Services, grew up as a Korean adoptee in the fifties and sixties. She came to the United States at the age of four from an orphanage founded by Mr. and Mrs. Harry Holt. Looking into her past was something she had not planned to do, for she assumed that there would be no possibility of ever finding anything. Also, she felt no compelling need.

"I never expected to search," Susan related. "I had not even seriously considered it. In fact, for a long time I didn't quite understand what compelled some adoptees to want to search for their birth family." However, as Susan reached out to help another Korean adopted person, that action impacted the direction her own life would take.

Susan visited Korea in 1990, attempting to locate the birth mother of an adoptee who required a bone-marrow transplant. She was successful in the search and met the young man's birth mother the following summer in Korea. That encounter ignited something within Susan.

> That experience caused me to reflect on my own birth mother and wish I could somehow reassure her that I was all right.
>
> In the summer of 1992, I placed a small ad in the weekly newspaper of In Chon, which is in northwest Seoul. The ad included my Korean passport photo and my Korean name. Within a few weeks I had a reply from a woman who said she was my stepsister.

In the weeks that followed, as more and more information reached Susan, it created new and unsettling emotions for her.

> My search was connected to deep feelings that evoked a wide range of responses. Each new discovery was attached to an emotion— excitement, anticipation, fear, sadness, happiness, confusion. I think my most defining emotion was fear. I was going into the unknown. I had no control over the process or over how it would turn out.

A portion from a journal entry written in the fall of 1992 reflects Susan's strong emotions:

> Dear Mother,
> I'm coming to find you . . .
> Perhaps what I really mean is,
>   I'm coming to be found . . .
> I'm so scared.
> What if I really do find you?
>   After all these years—
> How will that feel?
>   For both of us.
> I pray this doesn't hurt us—either of us,
>   beyond wounds that will never heal.
> I understand clearly
>   this is the risk I am taking

And I accept responsibility for that.
That's why,
I'm so afraid.

Eventually the news that Susan received from Korea brought incredible disappointment and pain, yet also hope. She learned her mother had died fourteen years earlier. However, she discovered she had two half-brothers who didn't know of her, but would gladly welcome her as their sister.

In August 1993, Susan had the opportunity to visit her mother's grave and meet her brothers. Of that period of time, Susan wrote:

I can't believe how hard this is. . . . But I do not regret that I am standing here above this tangle of weeds that is my mother's grave. . . . As time goes by, it is a little easier. I believe it will become easier still. The feelings will continue to move and change until they melt into a comfortable pattern for all of us. It's nice to see faces that look like my own. Not because they are beautiful, but because they provide a mirror for me that reflects our mother whose face I do not remember.

Although Susan walked through intense emotional pain and confusion prior to, during, and post search, it would be a journey she would not undo.

This experience was difficult. I don't regret having done it, but there were times in the process when I did. I could not have predicted the intense emotional roller coaster experience this would be. I was strongly supported by friends and family, but ultimately, the feelings belonged to me, and I was the one who had to live with them.

I believe the process of searching has great risks. There is so much that is out of your control, and it continues at an intense emotional level that is sometimes very difficult. I am still discovering what all this means to me. I hope adoptees who are considering searching for birth parents do so carefully, slowly, and with support from those closest to them.

This experience confirmed for me that family is shared history more than shared genetics. My (adoptive) family is my family—it's expanded a bit, and over time I'm still learning what this means to all of us.[6]

For the international searcher, running into dead ends or finding the death of birth parents are strong possibilities. Returning to the country of birth does help fill in missing pieces, as the adoptee connects in a broader sense to his heritage, culture, and ethnicity. The same experience can benefit adoptees from this country who find such disappointing realities at the end of their search.

Dr. Maguire Pavao in counseling adoptees in this circumstance offers a ray of hope:

> Those who find death at the end of a search, by returning to places of the past, may have the opportunity to learn more about their birth parents from those left behind than they would have if they were still living. They will hear both the bad and the good. What they find will have a lot to do with who they are as an adopted person, for the search is symbol of a search for self. The clues they find will be clues to themselves. There is really no such thing as a bad search, for the search will find out truth and truth is ultimately what one is looking for.[7]

A WORD OF ADVICE FROM BETSIE NORRIS

Those whose search ends by finding death, or a dead end, experience the lowest point on the emotional roller coaster of the search. Death or dead ends are so final.

In these situations, can a person achieve the resolution he started the search to find? We hope he can, at least in part.

Don't avoid the grief process. Grief is normal and healthy. Others may not understand this loss you are suffering, they may not realize that, yes, you have lost a very real, very important person in your life. Turn to those who do understand.

Don't be afraid to share your tragic story with your adoption support group. You are not the only one this has happened to, and others need to be aware of the full range of experiences. Do not shelter them and isolate yourself, even though this may be what you feel like doing.

Find ways to take care of yourself. Acknowledge the extent of your loss and give yourself time to interpret what this means to you. Gather all the information you can. Cry. Scream if you want to.

In the Adoption Network Cleveland, we have begun a tradition of sending flowers to members who find death at the end of their search. Our members have often told us that this was the most concrete, or sometimes the only, acknowledgment they had of their loss; this allowed them to begin the grieving process. Sadly, they were usually the only expressions of sympathy they got, as others may not have grasped how real their loss is.

CHAPTER NINE

REVISITING AN OLD WOUND: ENCOUNTERING DENIAL OR REJECTION

❖

It can feel like death to an adoptee

when the birth mother refuses

a meeting, as if only she can sanction

the reality of the adoptee's life.[1]

BETTY JEAN LIFTON

COMING TOGETHER

BY GUY GRAY, AGE 32

I do not understand the forces that keep us apart.

Nor the force that compels me to go on.

Maybe it's a seed you planted in my mind.

You told me, "Never. Never contact me under any circumstances."

You could have told me, "Not now" or "Later," but you said, "Never."

So now I look to "never" and wonder if I see a message. I often tell my wife, "No means maybe, and maybe means yes."

So perhaps never means someday. Maybe someday soon.

You told me I opened a Pandora's box by contacting you. I remember from mythology this was a box filled with terrible thoughts and emotions.

I read up on Pandora.

In her box were plagues innumerable, sorrow and mischief for mankind. There was one good thing in Pandora's box—hope.

I have hope.

You know, I'd give it to you in an instant if I could just find a way.

I know we are far apart. Just a little bit longer . . . it is in your hands. Look, I have come a long way. I am able to trust you now.

Denial or rejection perhaps stands as the greatest fear for any adopted person who makes the decision to search for birth family members. Rejection is an opposing response to a shaky, uncertain extended hand. Rejection is the dashing of a hope to embrace and to be embraced, to love and to be loved by the one person who has existed only within the deep recesses of the heart.

To come full circle toward wholeness and healing of the pain of rejection by a birth mother or other birth family members, an adoptee must recognize and verbalize her own depth of feeling. Often, unable to reach down far enough for herself, it is helpful to listen empathically to the feelings of others. A second step in the process toward healing is to look at the "whys" behind the rejection, for surface appearances fail to tell the whole story. The adopted person must step into the shoes of someone who perhaps has pierced her heart severely and examine the reasons why the arrow flew from the bow. Finally, she must learn how to deal with the issue of rejection and to allow the process to mature her and enable her to stand tall once again.

Rejection and Denial: The Result We All Fear

"Rejection is difficult," says therapist Sharon Kaplan Roszia, "because with it comes a loss of hope. The fantasy before the reunion allows one to hope for the best. When the search ends in rejection, one feels robbed. It is a shock." What does the experience look and feel like?

It Was Not What I Expected

"All of a sudden I realized that somewhere there is someone who looks like me, might sound like me, even act like me."

For thirty-four-year-old adult adoptee Teresa Schneider, dealing with adoption issues was something she had ignored. From a young child, she stuffed thoughts and feelings away about being adopted only to find herself facing them in adulthood.

Teresa's confrontation of the reality of her adoption is quite similar to many adult adoptees. Some look for answers in teen years. Still others, like Teresa, wait until a major life transition looms before them. For her, the death three years ago of her adoptive mother brought the issue to the surface.

Following this loss, the reality of another person with whom she was intimately connected by birth emerged. Finally, at age thirty-four, Teresa faces what adoption really meant in her life. She had two sets of parents. She had two mothers—one who had died, perhaps one who was still living. It became consumingly all important for her to initiate a search to find out as much about her birth mother as possible.

With the help of her husband, Ted, and two supportive friends, Teresa set out on a journey to locate her birth parents. It took over eighteen months, and in the fall of 1992 she found her birth mother, making her first contact by letter. Her mother's response was abrupt, stunning, and painful. It was a shocking, disturbing day when Teresa received the following letter:

Dear Ms. Schneider:

I was extremely upset that you contacted me. Do not, under any circumstances attempt to contact me again or any of my relatives. The only people in my life who knew of the baby were my parents, two friends, and my husband. My children know nothing of this and it must remain that way.

I do agree that it would be right for you to know some medical history. My father died of a heart attack at the age of fifty-eight, twenty-three years ago. My mother died just last year following a car accident. She was eighty years old and was in good health. I have no brothers or sisters. I do have a medical problem with arthritis and high blood pressure. There is a history of heart problems on my father's side. One aunt on my mother's side died of breast cancer when she was forty-nine.

There was never any consideration on my part to keep the baby. Thirty-four years ago, most women did not keep a child if they were not married. I will not send any pictures, and I have nothing to tell you about your birth father.

I hope this letter gives you the information you sought. Do not make any more attempts to reach me. I do not want anything to do with you or your family. I have gotten on with my life. You should, too. I hope that the people who adopted the baby were good people with love. I understand wanting to know who your biological mother is, but it must end here.

Martha Joanne

The pain Teresa experienced after receiving the letter was deep and it hounded her for months.

"I have had a great problem with depression and being hyper-sensitive to the treatment of others. This rejection has carried over into other relationships. I find myself walking on eggs and wanting to keep the peace at all costs—even to myself." Teresa's heartbreaking experience is not unique, for others have had similar encounters.

It Came As a Shock

When I was twenty-five, my mom told me about a search and support group for adopted persons. Without her approval I may not have searched, because I loved my parents and didn't want to hurt them.

After I received my nonidentifying information, it took me three years to actually go further. One day at the library I found my birth announcement. My parents had been married at the time of my birth. I contacted the court to make sure the record was correct and the court personnel took it upon themselves to contact my birth mother. She told them she didn't want contact.

At first, it was a shock. Then in a few days the shock turned to anger and disbelief that someone I had these deep feelings for would not return them. I had to deal with the rejection and understand that it was not me she rejected, but her own feelings. I have emotionally and spiritually matured and dealt with my pain.

—Bonnie Mullin, age 27

I Just Don't Understand

I am experiencing a lot of sorrow and distress when I attempt to understand why my birth mother and birth father have no desire or interest in even meeting me. Can it really be that hard to do? Don't they understand the pain they've created in my life?

I am thirty-one years old and I still go through periods of incredible sadness and depression when I allow myself to dwell on the fact that these people, of whom I'm a part, just don't care. I have been anguishing with this for over three years. What in the world are they afraid of? Me?
—Lynn Gaffin, age 31

I Have Waited So Long

I found my birth mother over five years ago. The last time we talked was about eighteen months ago when I called her on Mother's Day. She was short and abrupt with me. It's so hard, because it's obvious she doesn't want any relationship with me. Neither do my two full-blooded sisters. In my mind, I have been given up twice. I thought things were going well at the beginning, but over time she has gotten more distant. I feel so alone sometimes, because the people related to me by blood want nothing to do with me. I waited thirty-three years for them to reach out to me, but now I guess that won't happen.
—Russell Batty, age 33

Some Days Are Extremely Rough

Because I have four precious children, I deal a lot with feelings of sadness regarding my birth mother. Some days, if I allow myself to think about her, it can get pretty rough emotionally. We talked for the first and last time over three years ago. She told me she was forced to give me up, that she held me at birth and held onto that memory. But she just can't see me. I guess she has never dealt with all of this and it's too hard for her to do so now. I had dreams of a warm, tearful reunion with my birth mother, full of excitement and anticipation, but I guess that will have to wait. Hopefully, someday. Maybe.
—Janet Biggham, age 36

I Just Wish She Would Give Me a Chance

What I would like to do is to visit my birth mother and talk things out. But I just can't show up at the door. I don't want to force myself on her. She's told me very clearly that she isn't my birth mother. However, everything I've found, including talking with other relatives, disproves her

141

claim. I just don't know what to do—really rock the boat and go to the house or just let it go.
—Charles Schneider, age 39

I Just Want to See Her

When my search consultant contacted my birth mother, she was plainly told my mother did not have any other child. She had given birth to a boy in 1950 and he had died at the age of two. There were no other children. However, birth certificates do not lie and I know Ruthanna is my birth mother. I have no idea why she has to perpetuate the lie. All I want from her is just to see her, just once.
—Sarah Matthews, age 47

Experiencing rejection or denial from one's birth parents can be not only devastating to self-esteem and push a person into depression, it can create guilt. "When I first contacted my birth mother," Kate Burke says "and experienced initial rejection, I wanted to take it all back, to believe it didn't really happen. My first thought was that I didn't want to cause her pain and I did."

Shuffling through the many emotions generated by the rejecting experience can do one of two things for the adopted person: leave them emotionally stuck in anger, bitterness, and depression or push them toward understanding and healing. A major step in avoiding becoming emotionally stuck is to step back a generation or two into the societal context of that day. Within that backward glance are the "whys" a birth mother rejects the contact from her son or daughter today.

Why Birth Mothers Reject

Curry Wolfe, founder of Birthparent Connection and leader of Adoption Connection of San Diego, has worked with many adoptees and birth parents as they move through the search into the reunion experience. In observing a few rejecting encounters, she believes these occur for a number of reasons.

Mothers Who Carry Shame

"Many women still carry the shame and guilt of becoming pregnant out of wedlock," Curry explains. "The pressures of family, clergy, social workers, and society created the belief that women who were pregnant out of marriage and surrendered their child were worthless. Most were told they should never share the fact of the pregnancy or surrender with anyone, not even their future husbands. Many have taken those words to heart and are not able to get past those instructions and the accompanying shame when found by their surrendered child." When contact is made by the surrendered child, old feelings of shame and guilt rush to the surface.

Mothers Who Fear What Releasing the Secret Will Do

Another reason some mothers reject, according to Curry, is that they have never told another person of their surrender experience.

"A woman may be married and never have shared this personal information with her husband or children. This prospect can be extremely frightening. Many women fear their husbands will leave them, and their children no longer love them. This fear of loss can be overwhelming."

"I do believe that fear is the key element in poor contacts. It is much easier to deny or ignore than to face something that may be painful to one's self or others. Many times women believe that if they deny the contact, the other person will just go away. In most cases, that is not true." Fearing to tell one's adult family is part of the blockage, but so is dealing with one's family of origin.

"Some women never told their parents. They were able to mask the pregnancy. The fear of having to face their parents after so many years can be so frightening that they choose to deny or reject their child before facing their parents or siblings." Some women have been able to mask the pregnancy even to themselves.

Betty Jean Lifton, in *Journey of the Adopted Self*, writes:

> "A birth mother must make the baby into a nonperson to give it up," Erik Erikson once told me when discussing the complexities of reunion. "Having done so, she will have a hard time when that nonperson comes back looking for her." I thought of this when a birth mother confided to me: "I cut off my feelings when I was pregnant. She was not really mine. Her conception was her death for me."[2]

MOTHERS WHO HAVE UNRESOLVED ANGER

Some adoptees who have contacted their birth mothers have encountered anger. "I believe," says Curry, "that this anger is never for the person. It is an anger for a situation that was out of their control." This situation never really left them; it followed them well into mid-life and beyond.

Kate Burke also believes anger is not directed at the child but is directed at the whole experience of having to place the child in the first place. When the now young adult reenters the birth mother's life, feelings of being out of control resurface.

"Years ago, if a young woman had to give up a child, the message she received was 'You are not a good person,'" Burke explains. "We tended to treat birth mothers as 'those people,' or 'that woman'—shaming them with labels most have never forgotten. Not only were they shamed, but many were forced to make a decision that altered the course of their lives—forever—and left them with incredible sadness and emptiness."

When I Relinquished My Child . . .

My son was born over thirty years ago and we didn't have many choices. Back then, having a baby and not being married was considered nearly a crime. All those years there was a big empty space; a part of me had been given away. I never let myself get really close to anyone, afraid they would be taken away too. So for twenty-five years I never told anyone that I had a son, not until he contacted me and I had to finally tell. I was angry at first, not at him, but at the fact that now I had to deal with something I had quietly put away as my secret.
—Diane Davis, 51

When I Relinquished My Child . . .

I was seventeen years old and a senior in high school. I was quickly sent away to an out-of-state, unwed mother's home, given a false name, and told not to contact any of my friends. My parents made the decision to place my baby. I was never consulted, just told to sign the papers. When he was born, I never saw him. I was told that was best. I was angry then, and when he contacted me, all that old anger came to the surface. I didn't want to see him, not at first. He didn't realize that my giving up a child colored every decision I have ever had to make. I've felt immeasurable loss, incredible guilt over him, my family, and myself. I've dealt with depression off and on for years. I didn't know if I had the emotional stamina to face him.
—Dorothy Matthews, age 52

"One thing the adoptee is not usually aware of is the mental and emotional process a birth mother goes through when contact is made," says Curry. "She will most likely begin reliving the relationship that created the pregnancy, the pregnancy itself, and the surrender. These often are raw and untouched emotions she may find devastating to feel.

"She may start having angry feelings and expressing them to the adoptee, when she's really angry about what she's remembering. She may be angry with her family or her boyfriend (at the time) for not helping her when she needed it the most. She may be angry with herself for not being stronger and standing up for what she truly wanted—to keep her child. She may be angry that she was sent away from home to live in a maternity home. She may be angry about the loss of her teenage years after childbirth. And all that anger could manifest itself in anger toward the adoptee. It's important to understand this."

Shame, fear, and anger are three of the major barriers that block a positive contact between some birth mothers and their relinquished children. Knowing what to do with that experience can enable the adopted person to move through the pain and avoid getting emotionally stuck in anger and depression.

What to Do If Rejection Occurs

Rejection is a strong word. It does not happen often, according to Curry. Yet, for those to whom it does, the word sounds so permanent.

"I wish there was another word that could be used instead of rejection when talking about a contact that doesn't go well," Curry says. "Rejection is such a negative word and it sounds so final, when in reality, it may not be final at all."

Denying a contact with the adoptee will leave in its wake a sense of incompleteness because for so many adopted adults, total acceptance is one of the hidden needs of the reunion.

"I don't feel an adoptee will totally gain a positive sense of self if the contact fails," Curry says. "There will always be issues and questions that remain unclear if not answered by the birth mother. The feeling of incompleteness is one some adopted persons must learn to accept." There are, however, some practical things you can do in the wake of a rejecting experience.

1. *Follow up with a letter.* If you have not received a good reception to a phone call, Curry suggests following up with a short, kind letter expressing that you understand your birth mother needs time to process the contact. It's a good idea to give your name and phone number at the beginning of the conversation so that your birth parent has it for future consideration.
2. *Consider making a phone call.* If you made the contact by letter and received no response, maybe a phone call would be appro-

priate to explain that you are not going to just appear on the doorstep without notice. It's helpful to send pictures after this call.

3. *Realize that time is important.* Remember that as the searching person, you've had time, perhaps months or years, to process what is happening. Your birth parent has not. Waiting a year or even eighteen months after the initial response is an appropriate time to wait to make another contact, according to Kate Burke.

4. *Do not contact siblings without sharing this desire and possible action with the birth parent.* Many adoptees feel it is their right to know their birth siblings, but as pointed out by Curry, "not at the expense of their birth mother, her well-being, and existing family relationships."

5. *Put the search in perspective.* One thing all searchers need to realize is that they went into the search for answers to many questions, not necessarily a relationship. If you get some answers, it may be enough to help you put missing pieces of your life history together.

6. *Don't deal with the rejection issue alone.* Find and participate in a search group. It's a good place to find people who truly understand.

In considering the issue of rejection, Betty Jean Lifton writes:

I am often asked whether I think a birth mother has the right to shut out the child she brought into the world. My answer: an unequivocal no. As for whether the adoptee has the right to meet with the birth mother at least once to hear their life story: an unequivocal yes. As one birth mother said, "You can't relinquish all of the responsibilities for parenthood just by relinquishing the child."

Does the child have a right to demand a relationship with the birth mother after she gives him the information he needs? No, the child does not have the right to intrude on the life the birth mother has made for herself after relinquishing him. Does the birth mother have the right to be part of the adoptee's life? No, the birth mother does not have a right to anything the adoptee is not ready or willing to give. . . .

When adoptees, at any age, need to know their origins, those needs should supersede those of the other adults in the triad. No birth mother has the right to confidentiality from her child at the

146

expense of her child's well-being. As Dr. Randolph Severson points out: "All people who walk the face of the earth possess the inalienable right to know their history and to meet the man and woman from whom they drew breath."[3]

Yet, in reunion, we are faced with psychological rather than legal and moral dilemmas. Violent acts, such as having to give up a child unconditionally, can cause violent responses. The birth mother is as much a victim of the closed adoption system as is the adoptee, traumatized to such a degree that when [the child] returns, she may not be able to recognize her own.[4]

A WORD OF ADVICE FROM BETSIE NORRIS

I have seen many, many contacts that initially met with rejection turn out well. If you've experienced rejection at first, you need to give it time and show respect for your birth parents' feelings, but also keep trying. While this can be an overwhelming emotional situation, it's important to keep in mind that the "rejection" is not of you, it is of the past circumstances and the resulting emotions of the birth parent. There is still hope and often the situation turns around with careful handling.

Here's my advice:

1. *Don't do anything impulsive!* Check out your actions with others who are experienced in these situations.
2. *Wait the time necessary for your birth parent to process what has happened.* Each day may seem like a long time to you, but it's important to give your birth parent the time she or he needs to think this through and deal with personal feelings.
3. *Communicate clearly and make yourself available.* Be sure your birth family knows exactly how to contact you should they want to.

Remember, the goal of the first contact is simply to open the door. It may take some time from there.

CHAPTER TEN

SEARCHING IN MID-LIFE: WHAT ARE THE IMPLICATIONS?

✜

Since my reunion, I now have no doubt that my birth mother did what was right for me, and I have thanked her for placing me for adoption. My birth mother gave me two wonderful people. I call them Mom and Dad.

JOAN WHITAKER, AGE 41

Kathleen Schultz wasn't an impulsive teenager when she began her search for her birth parents. She wasn't in her mid-twenties anxiously awaiting the birth of her first child. Kathleen wasn't even in her thirties, busy with her career and raising a family. When Kathleen began her search, she was fifty-five years old, a grandmother, and looking forward to an early retirement from the teaching profession.

Kathleen is not alone as a searcher at this stage in her life, for some adult adoptees postpone their search effort to the mid-life years—forty and beyond. In looking at the unique issues for mid-life searchers, several questions need examination: *What are the typical life issues for adults in the middle years? Why didn't these adults think about searching prior to this stage in life? Why do some adults choose to wait until this point in time to search? What are the special concerns? What do they find?*

UNDERSTANDING MID-LIFE ISSUES

Someone once said, "By the time I am forty I will have something to say about life. I will have lived enough of life to learn from mistakes and have the maturity to make wise decisions for the future."

The forties and fifties are seen by many as the "prime time" of life. Careers are solidly established. Children are becoming more independent. It's the high point for earning power. "People at this age still have enough youth to be energetic, but already have enough life experience to be wise."[1] With the maturing years before them, adults in their forties and fifties face important emotional and psychological tasks. The impact of these challenges can be the impetus that propels many adopted adults to initiate a search for birth parents.

Dr. David Brodzinsky, in his book, *Being Adopted: The Lifelong Search for Self*, says that one important psychological task during the middle adult years is "generativity"—a word coined by psychologist Erik Erickson, which describes the need to leave behind something of yourself—the urge to construct a legacy.

Dr. Joyce Maguire Pavao, author, therapist, and an adopted person, says that "generativity" is part of every adult's life. It is not only looking ahead, it is looking back.

"It is a developmental stage where most adults experience a heightened interest in looking back to grandparents, to great-grandparents, to family history," Pavao says.[2]

According to Dr. Brodzinsky, generativity takes multiple forms from the passing of wisdom to children to creating works of art to the transmitting of ideas to the next generation. The desire to "pass on something" is not confined within the context of the family but involves a legacy that can be left behind by a teacher, inventor, minister, or mentor.

Brodzinsky not only cites the need to construct a legacy as a task for mid-life adults, but points to four other challenges for adults in their forties and fifties as outlined by Dr. Robert Peck, a psychologist at the University of Chicago:

1. Acceptance of the inevitable decline in physical prowess and greater reliance on mental prowess for life satisfaction.
2. A redefinition of relationships with others; they become broader and more social.
3. The capacity to shift emotional investment to new people or new activities.
4. An ability to remain mentally flexible and open to new experiences or new ways of doing things.[3]

For many middle-aged adults, a reexamination of life emerges as they contemplate themselves, their family relationships, their social interactions, their careers, and their leisure activities. It becomes a period, according to Brodzinsky, for "thinking about where you have come from, what choices you've made and whether any of your past choices should be undone."[4] Because it is mid-life, unlike old age, there's still time to initiate new relationships, change the course of one's life, and reconstruct old decisions.

As a mid-life adult reexamines the past, a very subtle change in how he views time occurs. As Brodzinsky points out, "The question used to be, 'How long have I lived?' Now it tends to be, 'How long do I have left?'"

The ever-growing sense of one's own mortality creates a whole new urgency to accomplish tasks left undone.

"Mid-life is the time in life," said Dr. Dirck Brown, family therapist and author, "where the realization of one's mortality becomes evident. There comes a time for one to come to terms with his identity."[5]

The need to construct a legacy, a changing perspective on the meaning of time, and the realization of one's mortality are all issues confronting adults in mid-life. With a sense of the clock ticking away, adult adoptees in mid-life begin to realize that perhaps only a small window of time remains to resolve their personal issues of adoption, which may include finding their birth parents. It may be the first time the adopted person experiences an overwhelming, intense need to search. A whole new burst of emotional energy propels them to open doors that had previously been closed.

Why Do They Wait?

One might conclude that if an adoptee waits until mid-life to consider searching, issues related to adoption have not been a part of their thinking. However, that's not the case. Thinking about their adoptive status and subsequent search appears to be more than a fleeting, occasional thought. What are some of their questions?

Does She Want to See Me?

I reflected on my adoptive status at least once a week, sometimes more. I wondered who I looked like and what potential health problems my children and I risked in the future. By the time I began my active search, I reflected quite a bit about the probable age of my natural mother. I worried that she wanted to see me before she died.
—Robert Kahn, age 42

How Could You Give Me Up?

I thought about my adoptive status on a fairly regular basis, but it wasn't an obsession with me. When I had my first child, my being adopted had a new impact on me. For the first time in my life someone belonged to me and had features like me. It made me wonder even more, Who did I look like? What was my real mother like? I also wondered often how she could have given away her baby.
—Martha Schilling, age 42

Does She Remember Me?

I often thought about being adopted—I don't mean that I dwelt on it, but it seemed the older I got, the more I wondered about my background. I especially thought about it on my birthday each year. I wondered if my "real" mother was remembering and thinking about me, where she might be, how she felt as the years went by, and if maybe she'd like to know who I was and where I was.
—Judy Tubbs, age 55

Adopted adults who wait until mid-life do not do so because they never thought about their adoptive status. It was very much a part of their thinking. So why did they wait?

Waiting to begin search and reunion for adopted persons in their forties and fifties and even beyond is equally as emotional and traumatic as for searchers of a much younger age. The reasons for postponing the search until this point are as varied as the searchers themselves.

I Didn't Want to Hurt My Adoptive Parents

*As I got older, I decided that I'd like to try to locate my birth mother. I
really got serious about searching when I was in my late forties. I made
the decision when I turned fifty, with the encouragement of a good friend,
that it was the right time. I was also fortunate to have the help of a
cousin when I started my search. My husband, Bob, was very supportive
and understanding, and I will always be grateful to him.*

*I did decide, however, to tell my mother that I wanted to search and
I asked for her support. She gave it to me wholeheartedly, and I promised
her I would let her know as things developed. I had always been afraid of
hurting my adoptive parents if I searched, but over the years I decided it
was my right to know, if possible, and that I wanted to do it before it was
too late.*

—Judy Tubbs, age 55

*I always knew in my heart that someday I would look for my birth par-
ents. I felt, however, that somehow the search couldn't begin until both of
my parents had died. My father died four years ago and my mother died
last spring. After the first of the year, I joined a search group and I'm
now in the process of finding my birth family. I just couldn't bear the
thought of hurting my adoptive parents, so I just waited it out.*

—Celina North, age 47

Adoption therapist Sharon Kaplan-Roszia finds that allegiance to
adoptive parents is a major factor in why many adopted persons postpone
their search. Some may believe it is an either/or situation, that to search
would be to lose the adoptive parent relationship.

"Many adoptees feel strong loyalty to adoptive parents," Roszia says.
"They would not do anything to hurt them. As they see their adoptive parents aging and facing death, they feel freer to consider searching. They
probably have wished to do so for a long time but have chosen to wait."[6]
Some chose to wait until the passing of their adoptive parents. Others wait
until time and maturity helps them stabilize emotionally.

I Had to Resolve Difficult Childhood Issues

*When I was a child, all my friends had parents who loved them and with
whom they were very close. I wanted my family to love me and treat me
as though I had worth and value.*

*But my adoptive parents kept me as an outsider. For many years,
I had been through verbal, physical, and emotional abuse, and in*

view of the fact this was the only model for a parental relationship I had, finding additional parents, my birth parents, wasn't high on my agenda.

There was always something deep inside though that reminded me of a loss somewhere . . . a feeling of being incomplete. Driven by the possibility of a positive outcome, I decided at age thirty that I would take the first step and get a copy of my original birth certificate. When it came, I was overwhelmed.

In 1984, when I was forty-nine, nineteen years after I had gotten a copy of the birth certificate, I was working for a major company. My life was stable and my emotional strength was such that I felt as though I could handle whatever came along. I had finally recovered from my childhood experiences. Also, I had no delusions about being related to rich and famous people. My goal was simply to find a family. If I found something distasteful or detrimental, I was confident I would not get involved. I finally went to the courthouse where the adoption records were kept. From then on I have been actively searching.

I waited so long to search because to delve into circumstances that have been a mystery and a dark secret ever since childhood promotes great fear in me. Also, searching requires great emotional stamina. There must be a commitment to handle and deal with anything one finds. Previously, each time my intellect posed the question in regard to searching, my soul said, "I can't."

The reality was, I didn't know how to begin the search, and I didn't have the emotional stability to deal with a frightening set of circumstances until I reached this stage in my life. Although I continue to search, I have never found my birth parents.
—Robert G. Smith, age 59

Adopted into an affluent, dysfunctional family, it never occurred to me that family life could be anything other than what I had experienced.

The consequences of growing up in a dysfunctional family and facing those issues necessitated such sweeping changes in my personal life that it was four years after I entered counseling before I could find the energy or the time to begin the search. I would have started years ago. However, I couldn't begin to search while I was still trying to form a workable relationship with my adoptive parents, even after all those years. The reality is that I went into the adoptive family as an orphan. I lived with them as an orphan and I am now an adult living as an orphan. I hope any natural family I have will be closer to "normal" than

I am. I expect to be at a disadvantage when meeting them because of my dysfunctional family experience.
—John Walker, age 44

Robert and John are not alone in waiting until mid-life to face the issues of their adoption. According to Roszia, "Sometimes it's the first time in life they feel settled within themselves. They feel they have matured enough to take the risk and to attack something that feels frightening."

I Just Didn't Have Enough Time

I thought about searching for my birth parents when I was around twenty years old. However, I got married and had three children pretty quickly. I was so busy, happy, and fulfilled with the responsibilities of my family that I just didn't have the time to devote to a search.

As the children grew older and their emotional demands became more intensified, I focused much of my energy in helping them. I just didn't have the emotional strength it would take to tackle such a big issue.

I put it away until now. The children are grown. My husband is nearing retirement. This just seemed like the best time for me. I know that now the chances of my birth parents still being alive are pretty slim.
—Rebecca Hunter, age 54

Right after I graduated from college, I took a teaching job, married, and had three children. When they started middle school and high school, I went back to get my master's. I have been so busy with my career and family that I just didn't want to take the time—especially emotionally— to deal with my own adoption issues. Perhaps it was my way of denial, but someday I knew I would search. I just joined a support group and have begun the process. I think I have enough energy left to tackle anything I find.
—MaryAnn Patton, age 49

I Didn't Know You Could Do It

When I was younger, I thought of my birth mother when I was in trouble. I thought she would come and save me!

When I had my first child, I began to think of what she must have gone through in giving me up for adoption. I'm sure it ran through my mind a lot. But I never knew you could, in fact, find your birth family. So I tried to keep my needs put away.
—Jackie Carter, age 44

My whole experience as an adoptee has been one of secrecy. I didn't find out I was adopted until I was eighteen. Then no one would talk about it, so I put it aside. I figured since it was all such a secret there would be no way to find out any information about my past. It wasn't until I read an article in the newspaper that I learned it was something I could do. I didn't waste any time in contacting a search group in my area for help.
—Richard Garner, age 43

These are just a few of the reasons for waiting until past forty to search for information about one's birth family. Many waited for other reasons, yet finally came to a decision to act. What finally motivated them?

Death of Adoptive Parents Left Them Orphans—Again

As some adoptees encounter the impending death of their adoptive parents, they realize that soon they will return to an earlier status—that of orphan. Dr. Brodzinsky says that the death of the adoptive parents may make the adopted person feel abandoned and longing for a replacement family.[7]

For some who vigorously undertake the search at age forty or fifty, it is simply that "they do not want to be orphaned again," adds Roszia.

They Needed a Better Parenting Relationship

Another propelling force is a negative experience in the adoptive home. Once the parents have died, they anxiously begin looking for elderly birth parents to fill in the gaps. They are fully aware that time is quickly passing and the birth parents may be gone. The search may be an effort to gain a parenting relationship they never had. It may or may not meet that need or expectation.

Their Own Children Encouraged the Search

As the child of an adopted person, some occasionally find themselves dealing with the same dilemmas as their parent—Who I am? What is my history? Many adopted persons are spurred on to search due to the interest of their children.

"Often the decision to search is encouraged by the adult children of the adoptee," says Dr. Joyce Maguire Pavao. "They develop a strong interest in locating medical information and birth family history and sometimes these adult children take on the searching characteristics of an adopted person. It becomes a passion for them too."[8] Connie Hopkins found this true in her life.

As my children married and became parents, they began to question the genetic inheritance they, too, were passing on. My second daughter saw a TV program about search groups and asked if I would object if she pursued the issue. She and her older sister drove to the state capital and got my original birth certificate. It was at that point, seeing my birth mother's name, the address of the hospital, her age—nineteen, that I began to wonder if she was still alive, and if she was, whether she would be willing to see me. That was in 1993 and I was fifty years old with three children and four grandchildren.
—Connie Hopkins, age 52

They Faced Their Own Mortality

Perhaps the strongest force in moving adoptees in mid-life to search, especially for men, is coming to terms with their own mortality.

"Men tend to defer these emotional issues for a long time in their lives," says Dr. Dirck Brown. "Men are less likely to deal with feelings and then to act on those feelings that are so tied to the search. There comes a time when men who once felt invincible begin to realize that time is ticking away. What they must do is something that should be done with no further delay. Searching and finding birth parents is one of those issues typically tackled later in life for men. There's a strong sense that time is simply running out."[9]

Many issues keep adult adoptees from beginning their search until mid-life. If you are beginning a search of people and places from an unknown past, special concerns regarding the search, reunion, and mid-life should be considered. Kate Burke, past president of the American Adoption Congress, a search consultant and an adopted person, suggests five.[10]

CONCERNS FOR THE ADULT SEARCHING IN MID-LIFE

A First Concern: The longer you wait, the greater the likelihood your birth parents have died and they told no one of the child born decades ago.

Sharon McKinny was completely aware of the possibility that because she waited until she was forty-eight to search, one or both of her birth parents would be dead. What she wasn't prepared for was that they had told no one of her existence. When she first contacted her birth siblings, they reacted with anger and disbelief.

"A searcher at this time in life faces what could be a unique challenge," says Sharon Kaplan-Roszia. "There may no longer be people around who can validate the adoptee's story. There is no one to mediate, and it can stir up an incredible hornet's nest."

A Second Concern: Because you are in mid-life, you have a lot of living to continue during the search and reunion. You must not allow the search to take over and control everything else.

Although he dreaded doing it, Richard's boss called him into the office. He knew that Richard was in the midst of a search for his birth parents and that it understandably occupied a great deal of his thinking. However, it began to occupy a great deal of his time at work with phone calls and office conversations. He had to ask Richard to put it aside from 8:00 to 5:00.

Kate Burke says that adults searching at this time in their life must keep the search in balance. "They must be able to find a place in their life to put the search, otherwise it can take over and control all their other responsibilities." [10]

Phil Lewis, an adoptee in his early forties, experienced an obsession with his search once he decided to begin.

"It became so consuming, so difficult for me. I was so impassioned by my need to find my birth family that everything else, including my marriage, became secondary. I spent every available free moment working on the details. If I wasn't searching through some information, I was consumed by two fears, that I wouldn't find anything out, and if I did, I couldn't handle it emotionally. Finally, after I attended a search group and heard a speaker talk about how to work through search obsession, I realized what I was doing to my wife and to myself. It helped me to settle down."

A Third Concern: If your birth parents relinquished you forty or fifty years ago, you may find a less receptive environment in which to search than the more open one that prevails today.

Diane Wellington, at age fifty-two, had searched for her birth mother for over two-and-a-half years. When she finally located her, Diane was surprised at the response. Her mother denied the faintest possibility that she was her birth mother. She asked Diane to go away and never return.

Diane was sure of the accuracy of her information. This woman who so vehemently denied she was her birth mother had to be covering up. This had to be her mother. Why wouldn't she admit it?

What Diane had encountered, without emotional preparation, was the consequences that adoption secrecy created and preserved several decades ago.

"The person searching in mid-life must recognize he is searching in an environment today that is totally different from that of his birth parents," advises Kate Burke. Bearing a child out of wedlock evoked such incredible shame that denial of the whole experience became a way of survival for the birth mother. That shame and guilt, in many cases, followed these birth mothers well into their seventies or eighties.

A Fourth Concern: The search and reunion will have an impact on your immediate and extended family.

According to both Kate Burke and Dr. Joyce Maguire Pavao, some adopted persons overlook this significant concern.

"For some, the search becomes an obsession," says Burke. "It is all they think and talk about. Family members who were once supportive become tired of hearing about it. I suggest that the searcher limit conversations with family members to ten minutes a day." If you are searching, be careful not to get narrowly focused in relationships at home. Work at informing your family members about issues of the search and reunion. Be open to their questions.

"The immediate and extended family members, in order to be supportive, must be educated about the search and reunion issues," says Dr. Maguire Pavao. "They must be educated about how normal it is for an adopted person to want to search. They must be informed about how important it is for the adopted person to know about his medical history, his background, and the people of his past.

"The family must be helped to understand that the search and reunion is a process that evokes an incredible amount of conflicting emotions." It is beneficial for the family to learn about what might happen during the search—like finding death or rejection or finding overwhelming acceptance. "For some, finding the good things, like unconditional love and acceptance, makes it more difficult to reconcile issues of loss. If the family is aware of this possibility, they can be supportive."

An often troubling concern for adoptees regarding the extended family is whether to incorporate one's adoptive parents into this process. Do seventy-year-old adoptive parents help a fifty-year-old son or daughter with the search? "Yes," says Dr. Maguire Pavao, "I have seen it many times.

"For real healing to occur, I think it is tremendously important for the adoptive parents to be involved in the process. For years we have given adoptees the message that you can have only one set of parents. Reality is they have two sets. Integrating both sets of parents into one's life is a real step toward healing."[11]

A Fifth Concern: You may experience major changes within your emotional and psychological make-up—changes that will impact how you relate within the family and beyond.

Prior to her reunion, Connie Stephenson was a real "people pleaser." She felt so incredibly inadequate within herself that she thought the only way to be accepted throughout her family system and with friends was to make everyone happy at her expense. Connie grew up and carried into mid-life this sense of inadequacy due to the feelings of abandonment and rejection that lay buried within her.

In December 1991, Connie initated a search and found her birth mother. Although initially hesitant to meet Connie, her seventy-year-old birth mother finally invited her to her home. As Connie visited with her mother, she learned the circumstances of her relinquishment. It was a picture far different from the gloomy fantasy she had cultivated for over fifty-two years.

Connie's birth mother became pregnant at the age of eighteen, just after the outbreak of WW II. Her birth father, a soldier, left for overseas with a promise to marry upon his return. Six months after he left, she received word of his death. She had skillfully hidden the appearances of pregnancy from her family, but now it was impossible. Her parents made hasty arrangements for Connie to leave the area and place the child for adoption. All this was done against the deepest wishes of her heart. In fact, she was never permitted to see the child and was never told if it was a girl or boy. She had wanted the child all along.

As the months followed, Connie allowed the reality that she was truly a wanted child to sink deeply within her. She felt herself becoming more confident, more assertive. The changes that happened within her not only called for changes in her marriage relationship and with her children, but even with her adoptive parents as well. Connie wisely sought the direction of a counselor as she worked through this stage in her life.

Kate Burke sees these changes happen again and again. "I have seen adoptees 'tap dance' as fast as they can to the tune everyone else plays. But in the months and years after the search and a good reunion experience, that person begins to like himself. He becomes more sure of himself and has a clearer self-identity. The whole dynamic of their life shifts." As mentioned earlier, this is a reality of which the immediate and extended family needs to be aware. "Even in a good marriage, this creates a crisis that needs to be worked through," Burke said.

Experiences

Recognizing one's need to search in mid-life and confronting the concerns

160

that mid-life searches create prepares an adopted person to undertake a life-changing journey. What have those who have walked this path found?

I Found Unconditional Acceptance

I found my birth mother and two sisters in December 1993, one day before my forty-first birthday. We met in January at my birth mother's home in Los Angeles. The reunion went exceptionally well. I felt at peace and so did my birth mother. She didn't stop holding me and crying for twenty minutes. I felt as if I were home from a trip, not home for the first time.

The only thing I would have done differently is to start earlier. Although I'm grateful to have found my birth mother, I feel cheated out of the last twenty years when I could have known her.

Since our reunion, our relationship grows stronger every day. We talk often on the phone and my birth mother is planning a trip to meet my whole family. I feel God has blessed me by giving me two wonderful mothers. I love them both.
—Robert Kahn, age 42

I've Gone on with My Life

My mother refuses contact, but I send her Christmas cards every year. It has been two years since the first contact and I haven't received a call or even a letter of acknowledgment from her. I do have an ongoing relationship with a brother and a sister. Even though it has been rejecting from her position, I would still do the whole thing again, because knowing the truth has been tremendously helpful. I've been able to put this behind me and get on with my life. It's made our adoptive family closer and I have deepened in my love and appreciation for them.
—Jackie Carter, age 44

I Feel Truly Blessed

I have found my birth mother, in fact, it took me about half a day to locate her, thanks to the group Reunite in Columbus. We had our first wonderful reunion in her home. It went very well—her first words to me as I walked up the porch steps were, "Well, my dear"—a big hug and surprisingly, no tears on either of our parts, and then just a couple of hours of conversation. She was willing to answer any of my questions. It will be five years this May since I found Mama "Irene" as I call her. I feel as if I have been truly blessed—things just couldn't be any better. Our relationship grows continually—we write every couple of weeks and call each other on special occasions.

I feel a certain peace and I just feel better. It's so wonderful to know she didn't hate me, that she wanted me to search for her. It's so much fun having two brothers after being an only child for so many years. Also, my adoptive mother was very glad for me and couldn't have been more supportive.
—Judy Tubbs, age 55

Adoption has changed so much in recent years that many adoptees who have thought of searching, but held back, may feel more free to take action now.

Generally, the more years since the adoption, the harder the search. So, adoptees searching in mid-life may need to be especially persistant.

"I personally find it sad," says Betsie Norris, "when because of emotional baggage from the 'old' system, adoptees put off searching until it is too late to find their birth parents alive. I would tell people who are considering a search to do it when they feel ready instead of repressing the need for years and then regretting it later."

Adoptees searching in mid-life should seek support and invite their family or other significant people to join in their experience as much as possible.

CHAPTER ELEVEN

SEARCHING AS A TEENAGER: WHAT ARE THE CONCERNS?

By the time I was fourteen,

I felt angry, alone, and left out.

All my friends, of course, knew their

backgrounds. They weren't adopted.

I didn't have even one clue.

Everyone in my world kept me

guessing. I just want answers

to questions I am just beginning

to think about.

RAYLYNN BECKER, AGE 16

Any adolescent, whether born into a family or adopted into a family faces certain development tasks. In addition to incredible physical changes, adolescents go through turbulent mental and emotional transformation. As their thinking processes deepen, they shift from the tangible preoccupations of childhood in which they focused only on things they could see or experience, to a view of life on a high level.[1]

Adolescents begin to ask profound questions such as *Who am I? What am I going to do with my life?* and even *What is the meaning of life?*

Adopted teens are no different. They struggle with the same questions, but perhaps with a difficult dilemma.

Defining who you are as an individual is a major part of being an adolescent. Like everyone else, adoptees need to know where they came from in order to begin to develop a sense of who they are. Because they lack the basic knowledge of their biological roots, teenage adoptees have a harder time trying to form their own identity.[2]

As most adopted adolescents struggle with life's normal transitions, they do so under the shadow of a history about which they know little or nothing and, therefore, do not fully understand.

Throughout this chapter, the diary of twenty-three-year-old Carol Wallenfelsz who chronicled her adolescent struggles will give insight into the heart cries of many adopted teens. As this chapter stops along the way to revisit her confusion and pain, it will also discuss a teen's identity dilemma, examine the stages of identity formation and the first signs of an active search. A visit with three families, including a look at teens adopted internationally and considerations for both parents and teens will conclude this journey into the search and reunion question for adolescents.

FROM CAROL'S DIARY: DECEMBER 30, 1987, 2:18 P.M.
seventeen years ago, mother, seventeen years. at 2:26 mother, you gave birth to me—december 30, 1970. so what are you doing now? i mean, does it mean anything to you that so many years ago you gave birth to a child? and here i am—wondering about you. it's only fair that you should be thinking of me. but what *is* fairness? who's to say?[3]

WHAT IS THE IDENTITY DILEMMA?

Rebecca's tremendous musical talent was the joy of her adoptive parents. Just like her adoptive father, Rebecca could pick up any stringed instrument and make it sing. Rebecca's confusion as she matured was, "Who am

164

I most like—my birth family or my adoptive family?" She could play instruments like her father and brothers, yet she looked nothing like them. *Who am I really?* she wondered. She had no idea.

Establishing one's identity is not something that happens only during a certain period in life. According to author and adoption therapist, Dr. Joyce Maguire Pavao, "Identity issues are an ongoing process, they don't just start in adolescence. However, the teen years are certainly the major developmental zone for identity formation.

"It's true that for every young person, they are trying to figure out who they are not—and who they are. They are trying to play different roles, experiment with different looks, and figure out who they are along the way.

"I think that for adoptees, especially when there is little to no information about where they came from, there is an awareness that they don't really have the genetic information to do that kind of sorting out of their identity. They are basing it on their family of intimacy—their adoptive family, but that's not necessarily where their abilities, interests, and traits have come from."[4] For some the struggle for identity brings about major behavioral changes.

Casey, age seventeen, was nearing graduation and trying to decide what direction to take in her life. Casey knew little about her adoption, except that her birth mother was a teenager living on welfare. Struggling with attempting to find some type of identity, Casey made some poor decisions. Just before graduation she announced to her parents that she was pregnant. In spite of their acceptance of the crisis and their support, she moved out into the apartment of the baby's father. She had chosen an identity on which to build her life. She would be just what she thought her birth mother to be.[5]

Settling one's identity is more difficult for an adopted teen. "For most children," Dr. Maguire Pavao explains, "the people around them are mirrors in which they measure themselves until the adolescent years. At that point they look in the mirror and see themselves. They become more and more aware of how different they are. I think it is a complicated process for adoptees during the teen years. It is at this point they begin to realize they do not know another person in the world genetically related to them."

From Carol's diary: January 13, 1988, 12:52 a.m.
it is 12:52 in the morning, mother. is it right that thoughts of you dominate me even when I should be getting my rest? i guess it just goes to show that thoughts of you do dominate me—even at the oddest time. how can i not be dominated? i'm dominated by the

face i've never seen, the voice i've never heard, the love i've never felt—yet, i live to please you; to be you.

should i be angry with you? sometimes i want to be, but i think i'm afraid of losing you if i become angry. isn't that crazy. i'm afraid of losing something that i've never had. i don't know if i'll ever be able to be the "me" i am. i'm too worried about being you, pleasing you, loving you.

How Is Identity Formed?

The family psychoanalyst, Dr. Erik Erikson coined the term "identity crisis" to describe the time during adolescence that teens begin to question— "Who am I?"

According to Dr. David Brodzinksy, identity formation is not as simple as Erikson's followers popularize. "Most of us don't achieve a uniform Identity with a capital I; instead we come to think of ourselves as different "i's" in different contexts. We might have an occupational identity, a religious identity, an identity having to do with interpersonal communication or basic values or other aspects of our lives," Brodzinsky says.[6]

To achieve an identity, Dr. Brodzinsky writes, "An individual must integrate these various aspects of the self with each other over different points in time. For the adoptee, there's another element. The self as a family member is an important component . . . but the adoptee has two families: the one she knows and the one she doesn't know."[7] How can an adoptee gain answers when she has been separated from the people and information that will give her those answers?

As an adopted youngster enters the adolescent years, according to psychologists such as Dr. James Marcia of Simon Frazer University, identity crisis can be resolved in one of four ways.

One: Identity Achievement

This happens when a person consciously experiences a crisis and tries to resolve it by exploring alternative roles. The identity achiever asks herself, What do I believe in? and then tries on different values and ideologies. After a period of time, she makes a commitment to a particular identity and a particular set of values. For those who experience identity achievement, this usually occurs in very late adolescence or the early twenties.

Two: Moratorium

This person also asks the question, "What do I believe in?" but for various reasons she puts off making a commitment to any particular path. Remaining in moratorium, according to Marcia, is not a permanent solution, since remaining is inherently destabilizing and uncomfortable. Eventually this person moves on to identity achievement or identity diffusion.

Three: Identity Foreclosure

This type of identity formation involves a person who looks as if she has achieved a solid identity because she's made a commitment to a set of values or a role in life. However, this decision occurs before the individual has really had a chance to experience a "crisis" or other alternatives. Often it is done in an effort to please other family members. An example of identity foreclosure given by Marcia is the individual who goes into the family business because it is expected.

Four: Identity Diffusion

This teen is a person who not only avoids confronting the identity "crisis" but is unable to make a commitment to any particular route, such as a career or set of values. "Identity diffusion comes about because a youngster lacks either a support system that would allow her to ask troubling questions or a parent figure sufficiently appealing to identify with. The child moves through adolescence unsure of what she wants, unwilling to confront the options, unable to identify with a nurturing figure because none is available.[8]

Dr. Brodzinsky strongly feels that the adopted adolescent who experiences identity achievement has grown up in a family that allows adoption discussions and helps the teen move toward a resolution about how "being adopted does or doesn't fit into an overall sense of themselves."[9] Gaining information about one's past appears to be a large part of the overall picture for identity achievers.

FROM CAROL'S DIARY: FEBRUARY 22, 1988, 8:41 P.M.
over the weekend, mother, i met a woman who, not long ago, put her baby up for adoption. she cried, "i'll never see her. i'll never see my baby." the tears, how they poured from her eyes and from her heart. mother, how i longed to reach out to her, but the moment came and the moment passed, so on paper i wrote to her: believe me when i tell you that your child loves you for i am your child and i love you.

i felt you, mother, through her, i felt you. i clung on to her to let her know that her baby loves her, because mother, i love you. every morning i look in the mirror and i see you. i seem to be at a loss of words. everyone says that i was so loved, so loved and had to be put up for adoption. that's hard to grasp. just because the woman so loved her child and still does, doesn't mean you do. i must keep that in mind. i'm afraid to get too close, to get my hopes up too high. you let me down once before, why shouldn't you now?

First Signs of an Active Search

Do adolescents think about their birth history? Do they have an interest in meeting birth parents? The answer is yes to both questions according to the Search Institute's study *Growing Up Adopted: A Portrait of Adolescents and Their Families*, completed in the spring of 1994.

- Forty percent of the adolescents studied wanted to know more about their birth history. (60% girls, 45% boys)

When asked if they had an interest in meeting their birth parents, about two-thirds (65%) responded affirmatively. The primary motivation for meeting birth parents varied:

- To find out what they look like (94%)
- To tell them I am happy (80%)
- To tell them I am okay (76%)
- To tell them I am glad to be alive (73%)
- To find out why I was adopted (72%)

When examining this list of motives, it appears that the desire to meet birth parents is more than an inquiry into personal history. It is also a wish to connect and deliver a message of affirmation.[10]

Many teens wish to give their parents a message of affirmation. Many others struggle with painful issues of feeling rejected, feeling different, and feeling isolated that perhaps can only be resolved by searching for information and/or eventually entering into a reunion experience.

How does an adoptive parent know what to do? Is information enough? How does one know it's the right time to initiate a reunion? What part should the adoptive parents play?

In her over twenty years in the adoption field, Dr. Maguire Pavao sees adolescence as a very normal time to do a search, at least for information.

Most of the adolescent population we've been working with over the last ten years were adopted into families who were given very little information about the birth parents. At that time, the adoptive parents probably didn't care about it, they just wanted their baby.

Now that the child has gotten older and asks questions, these same parents want help with those answers. As we work with parents and teens, we encourage them, if they have the inclination, to go and at least ask for nonidentifying information. It is their right to have that information. The child is trying to form an identity and he needs that information to help with that. Most likely, at this point in time, there's a great deal of interest in just finding out information.

For some, information about their birth parents, background, and their beginnings is enough. For others, the need is far greater.

Occasionally, a young person's changing and disruptive behavior, according to Dr. Brodzinsky, may be a search in disguise.

In making a decision to open a closed adoption for a teen, it's important to pay more attention to the cues of the adolescent, says Dr. Pavao.

If the parents go about opening up an adoption without the child's knowledge or involvement, it can also work in a very negative way. They may not be ready.

Behavior is the language of kids. Some teens are very verbal and can tell the parent exactly what is going on. But there are teens who act out in various ways. Some kids run away to other families as if they are trying on different families. Then there are children whose behavior is becoming more and more difficult and worrisome to the parents. These youngsters could be crying out with their behavior for answers and connections.

Kara, at sixteen, began running away. When she finally opened up to her parents, she said she was in a desperate search for her birth parents. She always went to the same places across town, a place she knew her birth mother had once been. She had the thought that maybe someone she would run into would know them.

FROM CAROL'S DIARY: SUNDAY, DECEMBER 18, 1988, 11:14 P.M.
in twelve days, mother, i turn eighteen. eighteen. so how have the past eighteen years of your life been? are you happy? i'm not, not totally anyway. happiness is wished for. doesn't it seem that way,

mother? blow out the candles and wish for happiness. when you signed on the dotted line, you blew out the candles. did you wish for happiness. did you get it?

eighteen years is a long time. in eighteen years, they've changed my diapers, tended to and kissed my scrapes and scratches, helped me with homework, listened to my excited chatter (that's when I discovered boys), they gave me the car keys, set my curfew and understood when i broke it. eighteen years is a long time, mother what have you done?

they tell me eighteen years isn't old enough for an adopted child to pursue the identity of biological parents. they may be mistaken. i'll find out for sure soon. when i find out, you'll find out. you'll know when i know. why should such a large part of my life be missing? you blew out the candles. i had no choice. why must i suffer?

What Part Should Parents Play?

"I believe that all adoptees search," comments Kay Donley Ziegler. "However, there are levels to it—some just think about it, some talk about it—some may take action and make specific plans to do it. Not everyone ends up in the same place, needing to do the same thing."

Adoptive parents can play an important role, according to Ziegler. "They can help their young person move from thinking about it to talking by being willing to be open about it." They can ask questions that communicate to the youngster that he has their permission to get beyond the silence of just thinking about doing a search to talking freely about his thoughts and concerns.

Kay Ziegler believes an important solution for the family faced with this decision is to join with the child. "Entering into your child's pain by tuning with sensitive listening and support can intensify attachment in the relationship. I encourage parents to analyze what is going on. If they don't have a healthy sense that this is normal for an adopted teen, they will get defensive and push him away. By far it is better to join with him, not in his hairbrained schemes, but in suggesting a family project where each one can take part in helping him find the answers he needs."

Another thing parents can do, Ziegler says, is start reading about the subject. Getting familiar with the subject as a normal and natural outgrowth of growing up adopted will set the apprehensive adoptive parent at ease. "Parents can also gain a lot by tapping into adoption support groups and learning how other parents have dealt with the issue. Parents don't have to go to war with their child over this. They can, instead, join their child in his battle, his search for himself."

Dr. Maguire Pavao readily agrees. "Parents, who feel the behavior is signaling this is a critical time, can give their child some mission to do in the search process, because that is probably what they are up to subversively. Why not do it up front and together and see what comes of it? In some cases, the fantasies are far more dangerous than the reality."

FROM CAROL'S DIARY: DECEMBER 30, 1988, 5:52 P.M.

i am legal now, mother. that doesn't really mean much. it's been difficult to enjoy my birthday. this has definitely been the best birthday and the worst birthday i ever had—probably for all the same reasons. thoughts of you have dominated me all day. i walk around with this label on me, mother, the label screams "ADOPTED." hushed voices whisper "eighteen years ago," "julia" "given up," "adopted, adopted, adopted." i walk around, like today, in the stores and it feels like everyone can see right through me and no one can see into me.

A Visit with Three Families

Making the decision to initiate a search for birth family members by adolescents is an important one. Many factors come into play—whether it was an adoption plan or court ordered removal (as in the case of older child adoption). Also, the availability of information, the age of the teen, and the emotional health of the teen are other considerations in the decision process. In the following paragraphs three families share their adoption circumstances.

Adopted As an Infant—Andrea's Story

In her preteen years, Andrea Mitchell showed little interest in the whole subject of adoption. She knew of the circumstances of her birth and how she joined her adoptive family. Her parents attempted to answer her questions, but the question of searching was usually avoided or redirected. They were afraid they might lose her. As she neared her middle teen years, Andrea began to ask more penetrating questions for which her parents had no answers.

As time went on, they noticed a dramatic change in their sensitive child's behavior. She became increasingly depressed and withdrawn. Attempts at getting her to talk were unsuccessful.

Andrea's problem hit a crisis level. One morning when Andrea failed to get out of bed for school, her mother, Cynthia, knocked on her door. When there was no answer, she cracked the door open to find her daughter apparently asleep. As she walked over to awaken her, her foot crushed a pill bottle on the floor near the bed. Attempts to rouse her failed. Cynthia rushed to call for emergency help and then her husband, Peter, at work.

Fortunately for Andrea and her family, her suicide attempt was unsuccessful. Following her recovery, the entire family entered therapy. The theme that consistently recurred from Andrea was "there's this feeling inside, like a huge, gaping hole that has always been there. It just doesn't go away. It feels like a part of me is missing."

On strong recommendation from the therapist, the Mitchell family initiated a search for Andrea's birth family. Her parents petitioned their local court for assistance and received valuable information. They then contacted a search organization in the area which specialized in such undertaking.

Within several weeks, her birth mother was located and gave permission for the contact. The family met her in a park, about one hour from their home. Since that day, Andrea keeps in contact with her birth mother sporadically. She doesn't plan to establish an ongoing relationship with her at this point in her life. In her own words:

Dad and Mom are my parents. They have loved me and cared for me. Meeting Patricia was the most important thing I could have done, for it enabled me to close the book on a past I never really knew. It filled in an incredible sense of emptiness that was gnawing away at me. I feel complete and whole.[11]

Many parents, like Andrea's, have resisted the idea of searching because they feared the loss that might occur. But they now see that the loss in other ways can be much more dramatic and hurtful.

Adopted As Older Children—The Carroll Clan

In September 1984, Chris, age ten, Solanna, age seven, and Mick, age five, entered the home of their adoptive parents Chuck and Bonnie Carroll.[12] The children, having been removed from their birth home due to severe neglect, spent three years in foster care prior to joining their adoptive family.

In most cases, public agency adoptions are closed adoptions. The birth family in many cases, has had parental rights terminated because of severe abuse or neglect or, under the threat of such an action, has surrendered their children.

172

From the very beginning we intended to have a closed adoption. We were willing to contact the family through the agency so that we could continue to exchange information, and we did. We even sent pictures to the children's grandmother to update her on their progress, but we felt it was in the best interest of the children not to have contact.

However, events caused a change for the Carrolls that led them to reorder their agenda regarding birth family contact.

Obviously, Chris, at fourteen, had been thinking about his birth family, because while away on a school band trip back to his home town, Chris called them from a fast food restaurant. Some of his relatives—his grandparents, aunts and uncles rushed over to see him. That event, followed by a series of contacts as a result of deaths in the birth family, really altered things for our family.

At first we went willingly along with the contacts, which included letter writing. We thought that maybe this was a good thing. The children needed to know as much as they could. But it soon became complicated emotionally for the children.

The children's birth mother was very grateful for the communication in the beginning, but eventually she began demanding things from the children, emotional things. It caused a great deal of confusion, a division of loyalties and a lot of guilt, especially for the younger two, who were in the early years of adolescence.

Solanna, who is now seventeen, expressed her own inner conflict: "I struggle with the feeling of 'do I want to have contact with my birth mother?' I have seen her before and she wants us to come and live with her when we turn eighteen. I didn't feel like doing that because she didn't raise me. I still am very torn about this. I feel that maybe if I decide to have contact with her, my adoptive parents would be very upset or unhappy."

After walking through the last three years with this dilemma confronting their children, the Carrolls feel strongly about advising other adoptive parents.

Chris was ready for the contact at nearly sixteen, but the two youngest, in their early teens, weren't. I think that if a reunion is going to happen with youngsters who are adopted as older children from a dysfunctional family, it is a good idea to wait until late adolescence, or even longer, for contact. We have regrets about what has happened. At a time in life when the children should be busy with friends, ball games, and studies, they are consumed with worry over trying to please both the birth family and us. I think they need the information at this age, not the relationship.

I feel that it's important for families to enter this process very slowly and with the agency as the go-between. Once the communication begins without the agency acting as the intermediary, there is no turning back. And for us, life as we have known it is over. There's been too much pain and confusion for the kids to handle at their vulnerable ages.

A Teen Who Was Adopted Internationally—
Returning to the Country of Origin

Jill Freivalds, joined her adoptive family as an infant. She was born in Korea, abandoned at a police station, and eventually taken to a nearby orphanage. At the age of seventeen, Jill and her mother, Susan, who is the Executive Director of Adoptive Families of America, made a life-changing trip to Korea. They went with the intention of finding out information, not looking for birth family members.

It seemed that Jill's interest in her background began peaking at around seventeen, and when we had the opportunity to go, we took it. I don't think at that point, if we had not had the chance, I would have fully recognized the need.

We initially felt that we would probably find nothing. We thought that most information would have been destroyed. What we did find was, in one way, no more information than we already knew. However, in Jill's file, which had not been destroyed were five pictures taken of her while at the orphanage. It was like discovering buried treasure.

As we made our way to the various police stations asking questions, I discovered that the whole process of searching was so helpful to Jill. She was able to hear what society was like for birth mothers back then. She listened as the policeman described what it was like to have anywhere from three to five babies a day brought to the police station. She heard of the extreme poverty conditions and the deep shame felt by birth mothers. She was also told that in those days there was no legal way to make an adoption plan. The birth mother was forced to abandon the child.

Although Susan and Jill both went with some apprehension and nervousness, the value of the trip was inestimable.

There have been changes in Jill's life since the trip. She had the opportunity to get acquainted with people of her culture and to revisit her particular heritage. The trip was magic. She stands three inches taller, is more confident, and much more confident with herself.

In giving a further word of advice for the internationally adopted teen and his family, Susan Freivalds recommends that the trip be a family affair.

"I wouldn't just send a child on a trip by himself. The parents need to be there. It is such a highly emotional experience and the parents will be needed for support. Being there will give the parents an opportunity to talk about the feelings their youngster is experiencing. There will be sadness and confusion and a sense of loss. It is crucial that the parents be there to help the child deal with his or her feelings."

Susan adds one other consideration to the internationally adoptive family. "A teen may expect his country of origin to be very much like the United States. The contrast can be shocking and overwhelming. If the family has the opportunity to visit a country, such as Mexico, prior to his own country, he will be better prepared to deal with the impoverished conditions he may find, especially in some South American countries."

FROM CAROL'S DIARY: OCTOBER 23, 1989, 11:12 P.M.
dear, dear mother,

i know you're out there somewhere, i know i will find out somehow and somehow i'll return again to you. believe it, mother, we made a promise to each other. you carried me. i survived. i am alive. i have life. we made a promise to each other. i am haunted by that promise. i look at women with dark hair, dark eyes, i search for you. is it you? could it be you? no, no, it is not you. no it is not. with every day chances lessen. every day you are further and further away. I will find you. i will see. i will not be blind to my anger. i will not be blind to my sadness. i will find you. it is going to happen. it has to happen. i have to find you. i have to find me.

175

Considerations for Teens and Their Families

Making the decision to move beyond getting nonidentifying information to initiating a reunion is a critical one for an adolescent. Dr. Maguire Pavao suggests the following as considerations:

One: Involve a Supportive, Objective Individual

It's helpful to have a consultant—whether a search and support group or a therapist acting as a consultant, not as a therapist. The family can have someone objective helping them with their communication. No matter how much adoptive parents "intellectually" get it and believe they are doing the right thing for this child, many struggle with it emotionally. They worry about what they will find. They are very nervous and protective.

Two: Talk about the Stages of the Search and What Reactions Teens May Encounter

Families need to be aware of and talk about some of the stages of the search and responses from others the teen may experience. Many searchers get pretty obsessed with the search. It becomes like a detective story. For people on the outside, it might look like a soap opera. For the people on the inside, it is real life. As the search progresses, it's pivotal to realize that the journey is as important as the destination and can't be trivialized.

Three: Be Aware of Sensitivity to Rejection and Feelings of Loss

Rejection, or what appears like rejection, and loss create great sensitivity for all searchers, and teens are no different. People pull back. People say they are going to call and don't. The birth mother and the adoptee are going through pretty complicated feelings.

Adolescents comprehend the loss issue, of course, on a different level, and it depends on the person how deeply they feel the loss. Teens conduct searches in different ways. At thirteen or fourteen they may do a search for their roots just for concrete information. In their twenties, they may go back and do it all over again a different way. Some teens are just not ready to search at a deeper level, but they do want to connect.

Four: Offer Administrative Assistance

Sometimes a teen may say he wants to search, yet a year later, he's taken no action. At that point, adoptive parents can offer administrative assistance—like calling a lawyer or writing the agency. Youngsters generally have no idea how to do those types of things. Parents can become the "secretary" for their youngster and do some of the leg work, but the teen needs

176

to feel in charge. He must decide what he wants to do and when, and must know that at anytime he can put the brakes on.

FROM CAROL'S DIARY: MARCH 31, 1992, 4:48 P.M.
dear mother,
     i haven't written a journal entry like this to you for quite some time—maybe a year. i write now out of a sense of obligation. i think. i am not sure. in january of 1991, i received background information on you and the adoption. i contacted them with the hope of getting whatever information possible. i remember receiving it. i cried—out of fear of what i would discover; out of joy to finally have discovered something. i had planned to write you after i read it, but i wanted time to process it and react rationally. so i waited.

When Carol was eighteen years old, she gave her name to a search group hoping to receive the help she needed. At that time, she was told she couldn't search because of her age.

On April 10, 1993, the search agency contacted her with vital information. On April 26, 1993, Carol spoke to her birth mother for the very first time. In her own words, Carol writes of her experience:

It wasn't long before I held the telephone in my hand looking at it knowing the woman who gave birth to me, the woman who caused me such pain and such anger, the woman who I waited twenty-two years for—was on the other end. I looked at the woman who conducted the search and who first spoke to my birth mother and I whispered, "What do I say?" "Say hello," she said. *Hello.* That seemed absurd to me. Hello? My first word to my birth mother was going to be "hello?"

Well, I did say "hello" and what we said after that I really can't remember. I do know I didn't wait long to say, "I love you."

What happened after that is something only a dreamer can dream up and only a miracle can make come true. Mary and I are so happy to be a part of each other's lives. I know now that stubborn streak does come from her. And my creative talents, my love for the arts—her too. My dentist was wrong, my chin comes from by birth mother, not my adoptive father. All those years I spent looking for a curly, dark-haired woman, my birth mother spent looking for a straight, blonde-haired little girl. But there is no question whatsoever we are mother and daughter.

My parents have remained supportive through all of this. They deserve the "Parents of a Lifetime Award!" I have tried to be sensitive and supportive of them. I realize this impacts them as much as it does me.

Although this reunion is a very big thing to me, my family remains my family, even if none of us look alike. My three adopted brothers are my brothers as much as any brothers could be and my adoptive parents are truly my mom and dad.

A Word About Search and Adolescents from Betsie

From my experience with adolescents, I would say that while many are at a peak in their adoption issues, only some are self-aware enough to know this. There are many reasons for "stuffing" adoption issues during this stage: Adolescence is a time when people want to be the same as their peers, not different; separating from family, the normal task of adolescence, is difficult enough without acknowledging the adoption overlay; loyalty and dependence issues may be at a high point, to name a few.

Many teens will not talk about adoption, they may act it out instead. Many will deny it is an issue if asked. There are multiple ways to address and work on adoption issues without focusing on adoption, per se.

The teen years may or may not be a good time to have a reunion with birth family members. If a decision is made to search, it is important that this be a family decision that everyone involved is comfortable with. In most cases, I would say that this should be initiated by the adoptee. Always, it must be agreed to by the adoptee.

SECTION · FOUR

Life Will Never Be the Same

✠

CHAPTER TWELVE

INCORPORATING BIRTH FAMILY MEMBERS INTO YOUR LIFE: CONCERNS, CHALLENGES, REWARDS

❖

It was so exciting when I first met

my birth parents. I looked like my

father—just like him. It is so hard

to explain the feeling of being

connected for the first time to

someone who looks like me.

ROBIN CARTER, AGE 28

The search and reunion experience changes life forever. Once an adopted person searches, no matter the outcome, he is never the same. Once an adopted person finds a birth family member, whatever type of relationship develops, she is never the same. The reunion experience has a far broader impact than just on the two persons involved, for it reaches far beyond them. It has implications for the adoptee, the birth parents, the adoptive parents, birth siblings, adoptive siblings, spouses, children, and others.

Once the reunion begins, it impacts multiple family systems and changes the lives of many people and many relationships—forever. That's why it's crucial to understand the dynamics that are a part of the reunion. For this reason, asking adoption professionals and adult adoptees to answer commonly asked questions will provide an extra measure of insight for those heading into the reunion event with birth parents or birth siblings.

Those participating in the "panel discussion" within this chapter are: Betsie Norris, President of Adoption Network Cleveland, Ohio and adoptee; Susan Friel-Williams, an adoptee and Assistant Adoption Forum Host on a major online service; adult adoptees from around the country, Dianne Bonecutter, Robert Kahn, Robin Litman, Beverly Perry, David Schmidt, Martha Schilling, Judy Tubbs, Paul Verman, Joan Whitaker, and birth mother, Patty Bybee. Comments gleaned from a conference presentation by Dr. Joyce Maguire Pavao, provide an additional resource for answers to those commonly asked questions.

QUESTIONS OF COMMON CONCERN

What are some typical feelings experienced by the adoptee in the early post-reunion days?

BETSIE: There is a whole range of feelings that comes with major intensity. After my reunion, it was euphoria. It felt like things were unreal, too good to be true. I was on cloud nine. That's one end of the roller coaster. There's another end of the roller coaster—a "letdown." You use so much energy in the search and become accustomed to the frantic pace of search activities. Once an adoptee gets all the answers, and the high intensity energy is no longer needed, a letdown feeling usually comes.

SUSAN: A major feeling I hear is fear. Everyone is very tentative and *very* afraid of saying and doing the wrong thing. This contact may be the most critical relationship-building effort of our lives . . . so we tend to take things really slow *and* really carefully.

182

BETSIE: I think that sometimes during the first phases of reunion, fearing what one has found and may lose again is real for many adoptees. This fear of losing again can lead people to be possessive and cause them to do things they might not normally do.

What emotional reactions can catch adoptees unaware?

BETSIE: Many adoptees are unaware of the losses for them, and the reunion experience unleashes the whole grief process from anger to sadness, and finally, acceptance. A reunion, although a positive encounter, hits many in the face with the realities of what was lost to them—biological connectedness, history, and for some the opportunity to have been raised by their birth parents. I had a good adoption experience and love my adoptive parents deeply, but when I learned that my birth parents had married and had three other children, I experienced that sense of loss.

DR. MAGUIRE PAVAO: When an adoptee finds his or her birth parents, they're often not prepared for the depression that comes with that. The adoptee thinks he has been depressed all along but is not prepared for the depth of the depression that comes. The better the reunion, the harder it is sometimes. Why? One reason is that there's the loss of the family history. The adoptee meets the person twenty years later and realizes that he missed all of his history . . . and all of his connections. There is real sadness about that loss.[1]

PAUL: As an adoptee who searched and found my birth mother over ten years ago, I still recall trying to figure out just why I felt so unsettled and depressed after having such a successful reunion with both of my birth parents. I have come to realize now that this is just a part of the healing of the pain and scars many adoptees feel from being "plucked and replanted." One encouraging word: With time the low feelings go away, for they are common to all of us who deal with this unique thing called reunion.

SUSAN: For some adoptees, real anger erupts that WE were the ones who were denied our heritage and the right to know our own history and family. We have to be really careful to recognize and deal with that anger before we jeopardize our impending new relationships.

As the reunion begins, what is one of the initial challenges faced by the adoptee in the new relationship?

DAVID: One of the challenges for me was defining the nature of the new relationship. My whole question was . . . who am I to these people? I struggled with being biologically related to them while being a total stranger. I grappled with the fact that I didn't know anything about any of these people, but they are blood relatives. It felt really strange. I didn't know what to call my birth mother. I didn't know how to integrate them into my life.

BETSIE: Defining the relationship and integrating the new people into one's life is one of the first challenges and the resolution doesn't happen overnight. For me it happened over a period of two or three years and at different levels. I would listen to pieces of my family history over and over again and ask questions about other relatives. A lot of integration took place just as I experienced being with my birth family over the last eight years, seeing commonalities, gestures. It just takes time, a lot of time.

SUSAN: Part of the connecting process comes as adoptees are often struck by the similarities between themselves and their birth mother or birth families. We can look alike, have the same mannerisms, the same bone structure and oddities. We're finally able to see ourselves in another human being and it adds a great depth to our own identity.

What are some significant factors that affect how the relationship develops?

Betsie: Every case is different, of course. What each person brings to the relationship will be vastly different. Positive or negative life experiences will impact how each responds to the other. If the adoptee is coming from a negative adoption experience with a lot of baggage, expectations for what the adoptee wants from the birth mother may be different than if the adoptive home was a nurturing environment. What adoptees had in the adoptive home can affect the outcome of the budding relationship with their birth parent.

Another factor is the type of relationship the birth mother has or had with the birth father and how she feels about it. If the relationship soured years earlier, leaving a lot of bitterness, meeting the child from that relationship may hold more complications, especially if the child looks like the birth father. How the mother was treated by others in the past regarding the pregnancy and how she is able to deal with that past are also key factors that affect the post-reunion relationship.

Susan: Not knowing what to do with feelings, like being overwhelmed, can affect the newfound relationship. When the reunion (first contact) happens, adoptees are often overwhelmed with feelings and emotions that we had NO IDEA were going to come forth and manifest themselves. The best thing we can do is give each other the right of free space during the reunion process. There is nothing wrong with asking for quiet time to reflect and process all the new information and feelings. In fact, it is probably a very good idea to take a little time out during the whole thing.

One of the biggest things adoptees say they feel is a sense of dislocation. It can be like being present in their own bodies but sitting back as a third person and observing everything taking place in a somewhat detached mode. This can happen at any time and it is probably an indication that our minds and bodies have gone into sensory overload. If it happens, it is not fatal . . . just take a few deep breaths and remove yourself from the stimuli and regroup. In the end, it will help the relationship.

What are some particularly unsettling or difficult issues encountered by adoptees in the reunion process?

BEVERLY: For me, it was knowing how often to call my birth mother. I had to back off a little. I felt like I was taking up too much of her time by calling her so often during the first several months of finding each other. I needed to talk to her, to ask her questions, to hear her voice and experience any other connection I thought was important. Finally I had to say to myself, "Okay, Beverly, she has a wonderful husband and one daughter (still at home) and you cannot be taking up their time with her." So I have tried to be more aware of that.

Another issue that makes me a little uncomfortable, was that I find it takes a minute or so for me to answer once easy questions, such as, "How many brothers and sisters do you have?" Before I would say, "Just one brother." Now I have to go into this story to explain and I never know if it's coming out right or if I'm saying the right thing.

JOAN: A sensitive and important issue to me was that I had to let my birth mother know I couldn't call her Mom. She gave me life, but the woman who stayed up with me when I was sick and drove me to school on rainy days is the one I call Mom.

ROBERT: The only difficult issue has been convincing my birth mother that I'm not angry at her for giving me up. From time to time it pops up and I don't know how to make her feel better.

DAVID: It's been hard for me to know that my birth mother doesn't want to tell anyone else about me. Although her husband is dead, her three children know nothing about me and she has asked me to allow it to remain that way, at least for now. What I am concerned about is what if she never tells and takes the secret to her grave. What should I do then ?

PAUL: One thing I had not counted on, and it has taken some adjustment on my part, is the difference in culture. I grew up in a middle-class family in a relatively large city. My birth family roots are in a poorer section of Appalachian country in Kentucky. We think differently, our values are so different, and our lifestyles don't even come close to matching. I have to work at really tuning into where they are.

JUDY: I haven't run into any difficult issues with Irene (my birth mother) or with my new family. The only situation I had to work through was with two of my daughters, and that hasn't proven to be a big issue. My oldest and youngest daughters have made it clear, in a kind way, that they do not wish to meet or have any contact with Mama Irene until their Gramma (my adoptive mother) is gone. They feel very loyal to her. I feel badly that they feel this way, but have explained it to Mama Irene and she understands.

As the reunion progresses, what are some matters that may require negotiation?

BETSIE: There are many things that require negotiation—like when and how often do we talk or see each other? When does the adoptee meet birth siblings? Does the birth mother release information about the birth father? These are just some of the many issues to work through. The important thing is to communicate about these things, not to operate on an assumption. If one person is worried "Are we seeing each other too much?" and responds by not calling, it can easily lead to real miscommunication. Two of the most important ground rules are to be open and honest.

DAVID: I learned early on in our reunion that bringing up the subject of my birth father was taboo. I still do not know why, but I decided to respect my birth mother's wishes about this and give it all the time she needs. It could prove harmful to our new relationship and I sure do not want that to happen.

PAUL: When I first met my birth mother, we both were excited and wanted to talk all the time and be with each other. It could have developed into a real problem with both my wife and my birth mother's husband, because we were monopolizing each other. I think it was an effort to recover lost time. After attending a support group meeting about reunion, I realized what was happening. I shared my concerns with her. She had the same mounting considerations. We both agreed to step back from the relationship and not be so possessive.

What should an adoptee do if she encounters ambivalent responses— warmth one moment and coldness the next— from her birth mother or birth father?

BETSIE: It's very important to talk about what one is sensing and feeling, instead of just assuming that one's birth parents do not want to con-

186

tinue in the relationship. Feelings can be extremely complicated. It's true, sometimes people don't hit it off. More often, however, this push and pull is the result of the birth parent's painful past regarding adoption. Some birth parents have difficulty managing an ongoing relationship with their child because of this. In these cases the help of a triad or birth parent support group can be invaluable in helping her or him work things through and establish a positive relationship with the adoptee.

DAVID: The response from my birth mother initially was warm and inviting. She wanted to know all about me and my family. We talked on the phone several times before meeting. We met first at her home and then on several other occasions. A few months into our relationship, her contacts became brief. She was abrupt on the phone and refused to meet me. At first, I was terribly hurt and concerned that this was the end. Finally I asked her. Reluctantly she told me she was convinced that she would never be the type of person I would want for a mother. She had failed me once. She knew, eventually, she would do it again. After I reassured her, the burden lifted and we are now able to talk more openly and honestly.

How much should an adoptee involve his adoptive parents in the reunion?

BETSIE: I think the first question is "Should an adoptee tell his adoptive parents of the search and reunion?" The answer is YES. To me, there is some irony about not telling adoptive parents of the search. Not telling them about this important life event is a loss for the adoptee . . . after all, they are your parents, and parents usually share in their child's major life events.

How much should you involve them? I think you should take the cues from them. Hopefully, after explaining this is your need as an adult, and that doing this is not in any way a negative reflection on your relationship with them, your parents will want to hear about it. I urge adoptees not to tell their adoptive parents more information than they are ready for. Some parents will want to be up-to-date every step of the way; others will want to take a back seat. I find that many adoptees underestimate their adoptive parents' empathy and understanding about their need to search. Most often adoptive parents are interested and want to know.

PAUL: My adoptive parents always knew that someday I would search for my birth mother. When I began, I knew that it hurt them and I struggled with being disloyal. I shared my feelings with them and assured them that in my heart they would always be Dad and Mom. After those moments of real honesty, they really got on board to help me. Dad even paid the court fee for me. I made a point to keep them up-to-date on my progress. I didn't want to toss any surprises at them.

What are some ways to involve adoptive parents in the reunion?

BESTIE: I think involving adoptive parents in reunion goes smoother when there has been some degree of comfort developed through the whole search. For example, showing pictures and information as it is found. I showed my adoptive parents my birth mother's high school picture long before I found her. They were part of the search, so it was a natural thing for them to be part of the reunion. I was lucky that my birth parents were also comfortable with this from the beginning of our reunion.

JUDY: A year after my reunion in 1989, my adoptive mother met my birth mother. I invited both out to eat. We met for lunch along with Mother's sister and two of my cousins with whom I am quite close. It was truly a memorable day—Mother took pictures of me when I was little to show Irene, who was truly happy to meet her, and everything just went beautifully. After lunch, Mother, Mama Irene, and I met together privately in a small room and talked for about a half-hour. We took pictures, laughed and cried, and did much hugging.

About a year-and-a-half ago, Mother's memory started fading. She is now ninety-one and quite confused. I am just so happy she was able to know that I found my birth mother, that she supported me and that the two mothers were able to meet one another. I feel truly blessed.

What should an adoptee do about handling holidays with both families?

BETSIE: (Jokingly) I have worked that out very well. I'm lucky that I'm a nurse and usually have to work on Thanksgiving and Christmas! Seriously, it's perfectly normal to feel torn. Many adoptees might want to spend the first holidays after reunion with birth family members. The adoptees want to get to know the birth family's holiday traditions. This can be a loaded issue and can bring a lot of fears to the surface. Since my reunion, I have spent every birthday with my birth family. Other holidays I spend mostly with my adoptive family. I think it's important for the adoptee to explain to his adoptive family what his needs are. It is also important to be sensitive to others' needs as well. Of course, it's easier if you all live in the same area so you don't have to go out of town to see one or the other.

PAUL: The first holiday after meeting my birth mother was Thanksgiving. I really appreciated my adoptive parents because as the holiday was approaching, they sensed it was a dilemma for me. They told me honestly to do exactly what I needed to do. If being with my birth mother on that first Thanksgiving was important, I should do exactly that. Because they were open about it, I felt free to make that decision. Now I alternate between Thanksgiving with one and Christmas with the other.

What about birth siblings—are there any particular issues that must be resolved?

PAUL: After I found my birth mother, she told me of three other siblings, two half-brothers and a half-sister. Up to this point, she had not told them about me. When they found out, one of my brothers and my sister were pretty angry at my birth mom for keeping such a secret. They were not ready to meet me. However, my youngest brother thought it was terrific that he had another older brother. We hit it off. I've had to come to a point where I realize that, hopefully, time will take care of my brother and sister's anger. I realize I just can't push myself into their lives. The revelation of me was a pretty difficult pill for them to swallow, I guess.

ROBIN: One might think that adults wouldn't have a problem with jealousy, but I really believe my newfound sisters became jealous, at first, of my relationship with my birth parents. My parents married a year after I was born and I have three full-blooded sisters. Since our reunion, and it has been terrific, my parents and I have spent a great deal of time together. In the early months, my sisters would not have much to say to me. Finally, I went to them and shared my feelings. That really cleared the air and now we are doing great. We meet at least once a month for lunch. I was raised an only child, so having three instant sisters has really enriched my life.

PATTY: One particularly difficult issue for newfound brothers and sisters is what is called genetic sexual attraction. It is something which may occur between people who are related by blood, but who, for whatever reason, have been separated throughout childhood and into adulthood and are just now being reunited with each other in person.

Most common among those attracted are brother and sister. This is the same thing you may have heard about in the papers and on TV when two adoptees who have fallen in love and plan to marry (or just one adoptee and a birth sibling) discover they are actually brother and sister. It can most easily be explained by someone who has been reunited having spent their years in the adoptive family feeling "out of place" . . . all of a sudden they meet blood relatives who feel as they do—enjoy the same music, drive the same cars—there is a sort of euphoria connected with finally feeling that you "belong." Enter the adult adoptee at reunion time. Though it does not always happen, that "attraction," because we are dealing with adults, becomes a sexual attraction. Virtually all who experience these feelings are upset and confused. The confusion certainly makes sense, and the fact that the people affected by this are upset by these feelings is due to their healthy knowledge and understanding of boundaries.

DAVID: For anyone who encounters this relationship issue, genetic sexual attraction, it's important that you talk about it openly. It's nothing about which to be ashamed. My best advice is to share your feelings with your newfound sibling, get hold of an adoption therapist who understands this issue, or tap into an adoption search support group that can help you. Just having the knowledge that this occurs occasionally may help an adoptee who is struggling with this issue and doesn't know what to do with his or her feelings.

Do good reunions really last?

DIANNE: We have developed a really good relationship. We do not get to see each other as often as we'd like. All of my siblings are retired, and I still chase after a thirteen-year-old and care for my mother. We call and write and see one another as often as we can. They are a joy to my life, and they seem pleased to have another sister. I still get a little crazy if I don't hear from them for long periods of time. It's just that insecurity of losing them again. Now that I've found them, I don't ever want to lose touch with them again.

We started a new tradition. I have a fall get-together. I invite my birth family, my dad's side of the family, my mom's side of the family, my husband's family, and a few special friends. Last year for our first one we had over forty people at our house for the day. It was overwhelming. I expect more people in the years to come. Everyone feels they are truly part of an amazing experience and family. I tell them they are each a piece of the tapestry of my life.

MARTHA: Because of our reunion, my life is fuller and richer. I have a wonderful new family with many loving aunts, uncles, and cousins. My mother's husband loves me as if I were his own. My adoptive family has met my birth mother and some of her family. Everyone feels comfortable and secure together.

Today, I couldn't ask for anything better. There has been so much love to share this past year, and I'm still on a high. My "new" mom is very much a part of my life and that of my family's. I never expected it could be this good and I'm very thankful for all the people in my family.

JOAN: My birth family is a wonderful extension of my family. Having both families meet has made me feel that we are now all one family. I feel a very strong connection with my new family. I now truly believe that as an adoptee I really am "special" to have the love of two families. I also now feel that I was not the one who was "chosen." Because my birth mom loved me too much to keep me, she chose wonderful people to raise me. I call them Mom and Dad, and for that I am truly grateful and wouldn't change a thing.

JUDY: The reunion more than met my expectations. I was thrilled that Mama was so glad to meet me and wanted to write back and forth, and more importantly, that she wanted to continue getting together. We are becoming closer all the time. We are very open with each other, and she is extremely understanding, loving, and seems very, very happy that I made the decision to find her.

BEVERLY: It was everything I prayed for, except she lives so far away. Our relationship today is wonderful and happy. I feel we are still learning and getting to know each other. I just feel truly blessed.

BETSIE: I have been truly blessed in all aspects of my reunion. My (adoptive) parents were very open-minded and accepting of my search. It was only natural for me to include them. My father even told me that if he were adopted he would feel the need to search, which meant the world to me. I really felt he understood.

My birth parents were overjoyed to be contacted. I guess I had so thoroughly prepared myself for rejection that I almost couldn't believe it! I had a hard time at first. I think I was more shocked than they were. It was a lot to adjust to, not just finding my birth mom, but my birth dad and three brothers as well!

It took a while for it all to sink in, but at the same time it felt natural for them to be a part of my life. The hardest part was going from literally knowing nothing about my background to having all the answers right there. It was really a shock. Although it was all welcome information, there was an awful lot to absorb and integrate. I don't know if I realized at the time, but looking back on the over eight years since I found them, I think it took me years to absorb it all. Sometimes I feel as if I am still absorbing!

I have a close relationship with them all now. Often I wish we lived closer to each other. I live in Ohio, my birth parents live in Wisconsin, and my brothers all live in California now that they are adults and on their own. I also have grandparents and aunts and uncles and cousins who are important to me. I had no idea when I started this how it would all come together.

Searching felt like the biggest risk I've taken in my life, yet I couldn't be complete without knowing. I'm glad I had Faith (Faith was her birth name).

What are some books and other resources that would be helpful?

Adoption Charms and Rituals by Randolph W. Severson. It is a poetic collection of stories, fables, and metaphors that helps families and individuals experience their circumstances from a unique perspective.

The Adoption Searchbook: Techniques for Tracing People by Mary Jo Rillera. This is a highly practical how-to guide of search methods and techniques.

The Adoption Triangle by Arthur D. Sorosky, Annette Baran, and Reuben Pannor. This is a classic in the search arena and is a considerate presentation of the effect of sealed records on the members of the adoption triad.

Adoption Without Fear by James L. Gritter. This book provides first-person narratives with adoptive couples on their open adoption experiences.

Birthbond by Judith S. Gediman and Linda P. Brown. This book aids the reader in understanding the emotions and circumstances involved in the post-reunion experience. It is crucial reading.

Courageous Blessing by Carol Demuth. This booklet offers helpful insight for adoptive parents as they work to understand the motivations of their adult child's need to find his or her roots.

Journey of the Adopted Self by Betty Jean Lifton. This new book brings insight and compassion into the life of the reader. It is essential reading.

The Other Mother by Carol Shaefer. This author shares her experiences as a birth mother and offers a poignant, honest perspective.

NOTES

Chapter One: Growing Up Adopted—The Unique Struggles

1. Jayne Schooler, *The Whole Life Adoption Book* (Colorado Springs, CO: Piñon Press, 1993), page 201.
2. Robert Anderson, M.D., *Second Choices: Growing Up Adopted* (Chesterfield, MO: Badger Press, 1993), page 21.
3. Personal interview with Linda Yellin, MSW, ACSW, therapist and consultant, reunited adoptee, January 1994. Linda Yellin may be reached at 27600 Farmington Road, Suite 107, Farmington Hills, MI 48334 (810-489-9570).
4. Sharon Kaplan Roszia and Deborah Silverstein, workshop entitled "The Seven Core Issues of Adoptees," presented to the American Adoption Congress, 1988. Roszia and Silverstein developed "The Seven Core Issues" in the mid-eighties. They have presented the subject nationally and internationally, have multiple audio recordings and a video presentation. Sharon is the director of Kinship Alliance. They are both adoption therapists in California.
5. Schooler, page 109.
6. David Brodzinsky, Ph.D., et al., *Being Adopted: The Lifelong Search for Self* (New York: Doubleday, 1992), page 142.
7. Roszia and Silverstein.
8. Anderson, page 31.
9. David Damico, *Faces of Rage*, as quoted by Schooler, pages 109-110.
10. Damico, quoted by Schooler, pages 109-110.
11. Sharon Kaplan-Roszia at a workshop on "The Seven Core Issues of Adoption" presented to the 1988 American Adoption Congress.
12. Merle Fossum as quoted by Lewis B. Smedes, *Shame and Grace: Healing the Shame We Don't Deserve* (San Francisco: Harper and Row, 1993), page 4.
13. Gershen Kaufman as quoted by Smedes, page 7.
14. Smedes, page 11.

15. Smedes, page 71.
16. Jody McPhillips, "Powerful Forces Lead Children on a Search for their Birth Parents," *The Houston Chronicle*, June 27, 1993, section A, 9.
17. Susan M. Barieri, "Adoptees Try to Fill in the Blanks: A Half-Million Americans Are Looking for Answers They Can Only Get By Finding Their Biological Parents," *Orlando Sentinel Tribune*, March 23, 1992, page D1.
18. Carole Wallenfelsz, "Missing Pieces," *Birthparents Today Newsletter* (Cincinnati, OH: Summer 1993), page 4.
19. Wallenfelsz, page 4.

Chapter Two: To Search or Not to Search

1. Betsie Norris, "The Impact of Secrecy and Openness in Adoption," as presented to the American Orthopsychiatric Association Meeting, San Francisco, California, 1993.
2. Randolph Severson, Ph.D., "Transformations," as presented to the American Adoption Congress, Cleveland, Ohio, 1993.
3. Robert Anderson, as quoted by Mary Ellen Butke at the American Adoption Congress Conference.
4. Personal interview with Sharon Kaplan-Roszia, February 28, 1994.
5. Robert Anderson, "The Nature of the Adoptee Search: Adventure, Cure or Growth?" *Children Welfare* LXVIII 6 (November-December), page 625.
6. Adapted from *The Whole Life Adoption Book* (Colorado Springs, CO: Piñon Press, 1993), pages 203, 204.
7. Brodzinsky, *Being Adopted: The Lifelong Search for Self,* page 143.
8. "Growing Up Adopted—What It Feels Like As an Adult," *Family Ties Newsletter*, published by Warren County Children's Services (November-December 1993), page 4.
9. Severson, "Transformations," as presented to the American Adoption Congress, Cleveland, 1993.
10. Norris, page 3.
11. Norris, page 3.
12. Mary Jo Rillera, *The Adoption Searchbook* (Westminister, CA: Triadoption Publishers, 1991), page 15.
13. Personal interview with Sharon Kaplan-Roszia, February 28, 1994, used by permission.
14. Interview with Kaplan-Roszia.

Chapter Three: How to Communicate the Decision to Search to Adoptive Parents

1. Randolph Severson, *Adoption: Charms and Rituals for Healing* (Dallas: House of Tomorrow Productions, 1991), page 101.
2. Personal interview with Anu Sharma of the Search Institute of Minneapolis, March 21, 1994, used by permission.
3. Miriam Reitz and Kenneth W. Watson, *Adoption and the Family System* (New York: Guilford Press, 1993), page 3.
4. Reitz and Watson, page 4.
5. Kaplan-Roszia, personal interview, February 28, 1994, used by permission.
6. "Model of the Myth" created by David L. Schooler, MPC.
7. Carol Demuth, *Courageous Blessing: Adoptive Parents and the Search* (Garland, TX: Aries Center, 1993), page 3.
8. Elizabeth Fishel, *Family Mirrors: What Our Children's Lives Reveal About Ourselves* (Boston: Houghton Mifflin, 1991), page 51.
9. Dolores Curran, *Traits of a Healthy Family* (New York: Ballantine Books, 1988), page 8.
10. Anu Sharma, personal interview, March 21, 1994, used by permission.
11. Fishel, page 60.
12. Curran, page 292.
13. Curran, page 292.
14. Fishel, page 59.
15. Dr. Jerry Lewis, *How's Your Family?* (New York: Brunner/Mazel Publisher, 1989), page 299.
16. Kaplan-Roszia, personal interview, February 28, 1994, used by permission.
17. Carol DeMuth, personal interiew, February 1994, used by permission.
18. Severson, *Adoption and Spirituality* (Dallas: Aries Center, 1994), page 17.

Chapter Four: Preparing Emotionally for the Search

1. Betty Jean Lifton, *Journey of the Adopted Self: A Quest for Wholeness* (New York: Basic Books, 1993), page 155.
2. Barbara Wentz, personal interview, March 1994, used by permission. Barbara Wentz is an adoptive parent and an adoption counselor at the Children's Home in Cincinnati, Ohio, and works with both pre-search and post-search issues.
3. Dr. Joyce Maguire Pavao, "Counseling the Adoptee: Post Search," American Adoption Congress, Chicago, 1992. Dr. Maguire Pavao is

the director of PACT, The Family Center in Somerville, Massachu-
setts, and is recognized internationally for her work in the adoption
field. She is also an adopted person who located her birth mother
over twenty-five years ago.

4. Michelle McColm, *Adoption Reunions: A Book for Adoptees, Birth Parents and Adoptive Families* (Ontario: Story Book Press, 1993), page
162.

5. Lifton, *Journey of the Adopted Self*, page 165.

6. Lifton, "Healing the Cumulative Trauma," workshop presented to
American Adoption Congress, 1992.

7. Rillera, *The Adoption Search Book* (Westminster, CA: 1991).

8. Schooler, *The Whole Life Adoption Book* (Colorado Springs, CO:
Piñon Press, 1993), page 207.

Chapter Five: Initiating the Search and First Contact

1. Allen Ravenstine, "The Lost and Found: A Young Woman Searches
for Her Source," *Cleveland Edition: The News, Arts and Entertainment
Weekly*, June 7, 1990, page 8.

2. Ravenstine, page 8.

3. Adapted from "Lost and Found," by Allen Ravenstine.

4. Jayne Askin, *Search: A Handbook for Adoptees and Birthparents*
(Phoenix, AZ: Oryx Press, 1992), page 27.

5. Askin, page 27.

6. Askin, page 27.

7. Askin, page 237.

8. Askin, page 247.

9. Askin, page 257.

10. Askin, page 276.

11. Askin, page 58.

12. Personal interview with Susan E. Friel-Williams via America Online,
May 27, 1994, used by permission. Susan, as a search consultant,
operates the nonprofit ICARE (Idaho Computer Adoption Registry)
in Boise, Idaho.

13. Curry Wolfe, "Making Contact after the Search," used by permission.
Curry Wolfe may be contacted by writing Box 23043, Encinitas, CA
92023.

14. Adapted from *The Adoption Searchbook*, by Mary Jo Rillera, page 184.

15. Rillera, page 185.

16. Rillera, page 185.

Chapter Six: Facing a History of Abuse or Neglect

1. Steven Farmer, *Adult Children of Abusive Parents: A Healing Program for Those Who Have Been Physically, Sexually, or Emotionally Abused* (New York: Ballantine Books, 1989), page 4.
2. Personal interview, May 19, 1994, used by permission. Marian Parker has been with the Hamilton County Ohio Children Services for over two decades.
3. Personal interview with Kay Donley Ziegler, June 10, 1994, at the Ohio State Adoption Retreat, Deercreek Resort, Mount Sterling, Ohio. Used by permission. Kay Donley Ziegler is a trainer/consultant with the National Resource Center for Special Needs Adoption and is the past director of Spaulding for Children in Michigan. She is a pioneer in the field of special needs adoption.
4. Personal interview with Dr. Severson, April 11, 1994, used by permission.
5. Interview with Severson.
6. Ronny Diamond works with Spence Chapin Services to Families and Children in New York. This was a personal interview conducted May 9, 1994. Used by permission.
7. Nancy Ward works with the Children's Home Society in Minnesota. This personal interview was conducted May 9, 1994. Used by permission.
8. Dwight Lee Wolter, *Forgiving Our Parents: For Adult Children from Dysfunctional Families* (Center City, MN: Hazelden Foundation, 1989), page 32.
9. Wolter, pages 27-28.
10. Adapted from *The Whole Life Adoption Book*, page 206.

Chapter Seven: A Walk into the Wilderness: Learning of Your Adoption As an Adult

1. The term "conspiracy of silence" was originally coined by prolific author and adoptee, Betty Jean Lifton.
2. Lifton, *Journey of the Adopted Self*, page 22.
3. Personal interview with Dr. Dirck Brown, June 13, 1994, used by permission. Dr. Brown is the co-author of *Clinical Practice in Adoption*. He is a family therapist and vice-president of the American Adoption Congress.
4. Lifton, page 23.
5. Personal interview with Dr. Severson, April 1994, used by permission.

6. Dwight Lee Wolter, *Forgiving Our Parents: For Adult Children from Dysfunctional Families* (Center City, MN: Hazelden Foundation, 1989), page 49.
7. Wolter, page 63.

Chapter Eight: When the Pieces Don't Fit: Finding Dead Ends or Death
1. Personal interview, June 9, 1994, used by permission.
2. Bruce Helwig, An essay: "An Unannounced Visitor." Bruce, a writer, martial artist, and long curious adoptee will complete his search in the next few years.
3. Dr. Joyce Maguire Pavao, personal interview at the Adoptive Families of America Conference, June 25, 1994, in Minneapolis.
4. Lifton, *Journey of the Adopted Self*, page 180.
5. Katie Lee Crane, edited excerpt from "Complete Searches," *Adoption Network News*, July-August 1993.
6. The sources for this account of Susan Soon Keum Cox's story came from the magazine and from a personal interview with her in July 1994.
7. Dr. Maguire Pavao, personal interview, June 25, 1994.

Chapter Nine: Revisiting an Old Wound: Encountering Denial or Rejection
1. Lifton, *Journey of the Adopted Self*, page 181.
2. Lifton, page 181.
3. Lifton, page 190.
4. Lifton, page 190.

Chapter Ten: Searching in Mid-life: What Are the Implications?
1. David Brodzinsky, Ph.D., Marshal D. Schechter, M.D., and Robin Marantz Henig, *Being Adopted: The Lifelong Search for Self* (New York: Doubleday, 1992), page 149.
2. Personal interview with Dr. Joyce Maguire Pavao on June 25, 1994, at the Adoptive Families of American Conference in Minneapolis. Used by permission.
3. Brodzinsky, page 152.
4. Brodzinsky, page 153.
5. Personal interview with Dr. Dirck Brown, June 9, 1994, used by permission.
6. Personal interview with Sharon Kaplan-Roszia, June 1994, used by permission.

7. Brodzinsky, page 158.
8. Interview with Dr. Joyce Maguire Pavao, June 25, 1994.
9. Interview with Dr. Brown.
10. Personal interview with Kate Burke, June 16, 1994, used by permission. Ms. Burke is the past president of the American Adoption Congress and is a search consultant in California.
11. Interview with Dr. Maguire Pavao.

Chapter Eleven: Searching As a Teenager: What Are the Concerns?

1. Schooler, *The Whole Life Adoption Book*, page 166.
2. Karen Gravell and Susan Fischer, *Where Are My Birth Parents? A Guide for Teenage Adoptees* (New York: Walker and Company, 1993), page 12.
3. The diary entries are the expressions of twenty-four-year-old Carol Wallenfelsz as a teen. She is an articulate young adult who writes and speaks on adoption issues throughout southwestern Ohio. Used by permission.
4. Personal interview with Dr. Joyce Maguire Pavao, July 1994, used by permission.
5. Schooler, page 173.
6. Brodzinsky, Schechter, and Henig, page 103.
7. Brodzinsky, page 102.
8. Adapted from Brodzinsky, pages 102-103.
9. Brodzinsky, pages 102-103.
10. Peter L. Benson, Ph.D., Anu R. Sharma, Ph.D., L.P., Eugene C. Roehlkepartain, *Growing Up Adopted: A Portrait of Adolescents and Their Families* (Minneapolis: Search Institute, 1994), page 26.
11. Adapted from Schooler, pages 177-178.
12. Bonnie Carroll is an experienced adoption social worker with the Athens, Ohio Children Services. She works with families on post-adoption issues.

Chapter Twelve: Incorporating Birth Family Members into Your Life: Concerns, Challenges, Rewards

1. Dr. Joyce Maguire Pavao, "Counseling the Adoptee Post Search," a presentation to the American Adoption Congress.

AUTHOR

Jayne Schooler is the Adoption Coordinator for Warren County Children's Services in Lebanon, Ohio. She has been involved with this agency since 1981, first as a foster parent, then as an adoptive parent, and later as a staff member. As part of her duties with the agency, Jane assists adopted adults with search and reunion issues.

In addition, Jayne conducts workshops on foster and adoptive parent issues both on the state and national level. She is a regular columnist for the *Adoptive Families Magazine* and has contributed over 160 articles to other local, regional, and national publications. She is the author of *The Whole Life Adoption Book: Realistic Advice for Building a Healthy Adoptive Family.*

Jayne and her husband, David, are the parents of two children, Ray, now age twenty-seven, who joined their family by adoption at age sixteen, and Kristy, now age eighteen. She is a graduate of Cedarville College in Cedarville, Ohio.